Outlines

QUENTIN CRISP

Other works by Tim Fountain
Resident Alien – The Play
Tchaikovsky In The Park
Julie Burchill Is Away
(published by Nick Hern Books)
The Last Bus from Bradford

*Manuscripts of Tim Fountain's plays are available from Ben Hall, Curtis Brown Ltd,
Haymarket House, 28/29 Haymarket, London*

QUENTIN
CRISP

TIM FOUNTAIN

Absolute Press

First published in 2002 by

Absolute Press
Scarborough House,
29 James Street West,
Bath, England BA1 2BT
Phone 01225 316013
Fax 01225 445836
E-mail outlines@absolutepress.demon.co.uk

Distributed in the USA and Canada by
Consortium Book Sales & Distribution

Series editor Nick Drake

Printed by Legoprint, Italy

ISBN 1 899791 48 5

For my Mum and Dad

Contents

If I think about my life

If I think about my life, I see it as a slow journey from the outer suburbs of ostracism almost to the heart of the world.

The first time I heard the name Quentin Crisp I was nine years old. I was in the playground of the school opposite my parent's pub in Yorkshire playing 'jellywobbles', with my friends. It was a rather strange game which involved the participants attempting to clamber round the stump of an old oak tree, via the extraneous roots, without falling off. One boy, whose parents must have had it in for him because they'd christened him Tracy, was particularly poor at this and, indeed, most other games involving any sort of bodily coordination. After his third unsuccessful attempt he fell to the ground with a clatter. At which point the 'cock' of Year Two, a lad called Savage, with a face to match, shouted, 'You're a right 'effin' Quentin Crisp you!' I'd no idea who Quentin Crisp was but I knew instantly what he meant and so, it seemed, did everyone else.

The year was 1976. The television version of Crisp's autobiography *The Naked Civil Servant* had just been broadcast on national TV with John Hurt in the lead and overnight the word homosexuality and the name Quentin Crisp had become synonymous. Neither I nor, I suspect, many of my friends had ever watched the programme but its impact was so great on everyone who had seen it that word had spread. The show, which the TV Critic Nancy Banks-Smith said had 'alone justified the existence of television', had brought the subject of homosexuality unannounced into the nation's living rooms and catapulted an eccentric 68-year-old artist's model from near obscurity to international fame.

For the next 20 years I don't recall thinking much more about Mr Crisp. I saw him occasionally on TV chat shows and read newspaper articles on his eccentric New York life in his famously filthy one-room flat that he refused to clean declaring that 'after the first four years the dust doesn't get any worse it's just a question of not losing your nerve'; but that was it. Then I went on holiday from Gatwick Airport in the mid-nineties and saw a copy of his *New York Diaries, Resident Alien* in the bookshop. I'm not absolutely sure why I bought it — I'd never read his other, more famous, earlier books and knew little about him beyond these fleeting media glances.

I couldn't put the book down: by turns, it fascinated and infuriated me. The story of his New York existence and his observations on the business of living there took me from thinking him a genuine radical to being a self-loathing reactionary old queer, and that was often in the same sentence. I was amazed at his absolute unwillingness to toe the line, even when I wanted him to. I remember vaguely thinking at the time how good it would be to try and turn the diaries into a play, but I'd just come out of a bruising dramatic encounter with the composer Tchaikovsky in which Pyotr Ilich had definitely come out on top and decided plays about 'real' people weren't for me. So, on my return from holiday, the book went on the bookshelf alongside the *The Orton Diaries* and Delia Smith's *Cooking For One*, where it sat, fittingly, gathering dust for the next four years.

That was until January 1999 when I had lunch with Mike Bradwell, the founder of Hull Truck Theatre Company and Artistic Director of the Bush Theatre in London, and the performer and founder of The Bloolips drag troupe, Bette Bourne. I was Literary Manager of the theatre at the time and Mike and I wanted to work with Bette and we were trying to find a project for him. We'd gone through various ideas: the story of his life — already done, sort of, in *The Dish* by Paul Hallam; old plays — rejected as the Bush only produces new work; plays by some of his American friends — 'too East Village'. We were beginning to lose hope. Mike decided to go back to the subterranean Bush Theatre offices and left us to have the pudding (future producers note: Mr Bourne always has the pudding). Anyway, I can't quite remember how it came up, but suddenly Bette did a little impression of Quentin, in that instantly recognisable nasal twang, and I creased up laughing. When I got back at the office I said, 'What about Quentin Crisp?' Mike, to his eternal credit, immediately said, 'Yes.'

Bette, however, was far from convinced. John Hurt had been so memorable in *The Naked Civil Servant*, and the film itself had been so famous, what was there to be gained from 'doing him' again? We tried valiantly to change Bette's mind. We were convinced that although physically he was unlike Quentin and although he had very different attitudes to life, they shared one crucial thing. They had both once been someone else: Quentin was Denis Pratt, struggling commercial artist, and Bette had been ... (he'd never forgive me if I told you). Both had reached a point in their lives when they had decided they no longer wished to be their old names and old selves and wanted to make a statement to the world via new identities. They had consciously reinvented themselves as openly effeminate homosexuals. Their artificiality had become their reality; their essence was to some extent embodied in their veneer. Eventually we wore Bette down, and he agreed to phone Quentin to ask his permission. (Apparently, the conversation went something like this: Bette, 'They want me to do you dear'; Quentin, 'Oh, that would be fun.')

Early the next week, I sent Quentin a letter asking him to confirm in writing the conversaton that he'd had with Bette. Quentin wrote back saying: 'I give my permission for Mr Bourne to impersonate me fully and for as long as he likes, yours Quentin Crisp.' We were on. It was at this point that I realised I had only read *Resident Alien* and had never seen or read *The Naked Civil Servant*, or his one-man show or read any of his other books. Suddenly a wild idea over lunch had become a reality. I was up to my neck in it. I decided the most important thing was first to visit Quentin.

In March 1999, Bette Bourne, Nathan Evans and I left Heathrow airport for New York, a city I had never visited. On the seven-hour flight Bette prepared me for our meeting with Mr Crisp: 'Don't try and keep up with him, just let him do the talking, just put the penny in the slot and let him go.' I took it with a pinch of salt. He couldn't really dominate the conversation so much could he?

On Thursday 11 March, in snow and with the temperature well below freezing, we walked down East Fourth Street past New York Theatre Workshop, across Second Avenue to East Third Street to meet Quentin. When we got to the corner of the street at Second Avenue, Bette rang him from the phone box. (This was a necessity as the electricity in his building was so weak it could no longer power the doorbell.) Quentin answered with his trademark – 'ohhhh yesss?' – and two minutes later we were at the top of the steps, opposite the Hell's Angels' chapter, leading to his front door. Then it opened and a 90-year-old icon appeared.

He was wearing his favourite fedora hat with a silk scarf fastened at his neck. He sported a neatly pressed pair of trousers and rather dainty black shoes; a 'Stars and Stripes' broach was fastened on his lapel, close to his heart. It was an image as familiar as the logo for Coca-Cola and yet seemed strangely unreal, it was almost too expected to be credible. Bette introduced me and I nervously shook his hand. He bowed his head, apologised for how slowly he would ascend the stairs of the 'last rooming house in New York', as he loved to call it, and then proceeded to sprint up them so fast that by the time he was on the landing he was out of breath and clearly in pain: 'blessed angina' he told us. Bette shook his head. He then opened the door to the room which had been the inspiration to a generation of bedsit bachelors and perhaps the most famous 'studio flat' in the world. Not even a lifetime of quotes about his hatred of domestic chores could have prepared me for what I saw.

There was a narrow corridor of no more than ten feet in length and about four-feet wide. Halfway down was a set of drawers totally covered in old make-up bottles and lotions of many kinds. The wall had a thick black train running the length of it – from hand grease. At the bottom of the corridor, directly in front of me, was a single bed up against the wall. At the foot of the bed were neck scarves, perhaps 50 or 60 in total, piled on top of one another. Opposite the bed, no more than eight feet away, were two small windows, with filthy net curtains hung at them. Beneath that was a Baby Belling stove absolutely thick with dirt and grime. In the middle of the two windows a piece of paper with the words 'Reserved Quentin Crisp' written on it, perhaps a memento from some opening-night film gala. On the right-hand side of the room there was a sink, again coated in filth, and a set of shelves complete with books, packets of dubious looking potions, old photos and tins of beans. The towel above the sink was indescribably filthy. The floor was utterly covered in books, papers and piles of possessions. Alongside his bed there was a naked bulb in a broken lamp, the crossword page of *The New York Times* with his magnifying glass on top of it, and an alarm clock ticking loudly.

Quentin led the way and sat on the bed, inviting me to sit next to him. Bette sat opposite us on an armchair no more than two feet away. The chair had a neat little coloured blanket covering its frayed arms which Quentin said had been given to him, like so much in the room, as a gift. Even his clothes were cast-offs he said. 'I am like a hospital, entirely dependent on voluntary contributions.' Sat together like this, Bette said we looked like 'three men in a tub'.

I nervously asked Quentin if he would mind me recording our conversation. (I was so green: it took me until halfway through the conversation to ask if he would mind me turning on the video camera, at which point he positively perked up and repositioned himself to be in the centre of the image!) He agreed to my request and the conversation began. I started by asking him what his reaction had been when Bette phoned him to ask if he could play him. He said, 'I took it calmly because a number of years ago a man at the Edinburgh Festival impersonated me and in order to publicise his show he donned a blue wig and walked through the streets of Edinburgh and he was attacked!' Quentin rolled about on the bed with delight at this. I knew immediately that this was going to be some afternoon.

The conversation progressed: England had been a 'terrible place' and he had longed to leave it; America was 'more like the movies than he'd ever dreamed'; politics were 'the art of making the inevitable a matter of wise human choice'; getting into 'a narrow double bed with a wide single man' was to be avoided; Princess Diana was 'trash and got what she deserved'; the life of a homosexual was 'so horrible', not because of the 'social persecution', but because of 'what you're expected to do. Does anyone really want to take someone's penis in their mouth? It's so disgusting I couldn't bare it'; and, even more controversially, he asked why Mr Clinton was 'sending the brave and the beautiful to Yugoslavia; let them die, they're only Europeans'. In the next breath he was telling me we must give our love to the underdog and the unlovable.

It was a breathtaking and fantastically contradictory display, delivered with huge generosity and charm, never once seeming belligerent or hectoring despite the strength of many of the opinions. It was made all the more amazing for me because I had never seen his one-man show and not yet read his books in sufficient detail to know that often he was quoting from them and had said many of these things a thousand times before – and he would have given this performance to any of the strangers who had called him up from the New York phone book and taken advantage of what he himself called his 'infinite availability'. (He never removed his name from the phone book from the day he got a phone to the day he died: 'What is the use of a phone if my number is unlisted, it means no-one will ever be able to call me, think of the expense.') The whole thing was delivered as if he was freshly minting it. It was spellbinding and lasted for over two hours. At one point he asked me if I would like a drink and he went under the sink and pulled out some brandy from behind a bag of rotting potatoes before pouring it into a mug in which the grease rose up like a fried egg on the top.

Later we took him to lunch in Cafe 99 (his favourite, Cooper Square Diner, was closed for renovation). There he proceeded to sit in the window (I later learnt he got a free meal if he sat there) and amazed passers-by who pointed. Even then his energy was undimmed and he continued to give us his views on everything with the vigour of an 18-year-old evangelist: 'I wish sex would go away, if it did, just think of all the free time we'd have.' At around 6 p.m. I walked him back through the snow to his room. It was slippy underfoot and I put my arm through his as we walked down Second Avenue. On the way we called into a shop where he chatted briefly to the staff and bought a tiny bottle of orange juice. When we got to his building I thanked him. He said he had enjoyed himself, shook my hand and then tiptoed down the steps and pulled his keys from his pocket. The door slammed shut. It would be the last time I saw Quentin Crisp alive.

When I returned to England I began to try and make sense of my trip and what he had told me. Despite all my attempts to probe him, to get under his skin, he had steadfastly refused to reveal anything that was 'off-message'. At one point, when he had told me there had been 'no times since he came to America when he had been unhappy', I had said I didn't believe him and replied that there must have been times when he was 'less than happy'. There was a long pause before he said, 'Let's say there were times when I was neutral.' Luckily I had the audio tape and the video footage and was able to replay the conversation many times.

When I did so I reached the conclusion that, despite his assertion that he only 'said things because he meant them', there was often an elaborate double and treble bluff at play in the conversation. Sometimes he appeared to say things because it was absolutely what he meant; sometimes he said them because he meant the opposite; and at other times I felt he was saying things to simply illicit a response from me. I began to try and understand why he did this and to figure out who he was and, more importantly, why he was. Was he merely the homophobe's favourite homosexual or actually a genuine radical way ahead of his time? Was he serious when he said he wished he had been born a woman? How did this creature, who Peter York described as 'quite literally an alien from another planet', create himself? How did an unknown artist's model who had written a string of unsuccessful novels, plays and articles in a squalid bedsit suddenly write a bestselling book, that went on to become a hugely influential film in his late-60s?

I started to look back through his writings and life. His works before *The Naked Civil Servant* were largely undistinguished and, by his own admission, not very good. Not surprisingly texts like *Colour in Display*, a book on window dressing published in 1938, found a rather limited readership and his attempts at movie scripts and stage plays fell on similar stony ground. However, following the publication of *The Naked Civil Servant*, his writings found a much larger audience – though, contrary to popular assumption, none, apart from *The Naked Civil Servant*, was ever a bestseller. They included: *How To Have A Life-Style*, published in 1975, a book in which he gives his readers witty and sardonic tips on living happy and fulfilled lives; *How To*

Become A Virgin, published in 1981, which tells the story of his emigration to New York in the late seventies; *The Wit And Wisdom of Quentin Crisp*, published in 1985, essentially a compendium of Crispian aphorisms; and his final book, *Resident Alien, The New York Diaries*, published in 1997, which documented his life in the New York social scene which he once famously described as allowing him to live for free, providing he only consumed peanuts and champagne. As well as the books there were large amounts of journalism and film reviewing. He regularly wrote a column for *The Manchester Guardian*, as he insisted on calling it, and for many years he was Film Critic of both *The New York Native* and the *Christopher Street* magazine for whom he also wrote a regular diary. Alongside his journalism there was his hugely successful one-man show, *An Evening With Quentin Crisp*, which enjoyed a good run in London's West End in the late seventies and which he went on performing right up until the end of his life. There was also an acting career which kept him financially afloat, not least because he always made sure he got all his medical treatment carried out whilst under the movie studios' insurance policies. His numerous film appearances ranged from cameos in films like *Philadelphia* with Tom Hanks, to major parts such as Elizabeth I in Sally Potter's 1993 film, *Orlando*. There were also countless appearances on TV chat shows and in documentaries, like Jonathan Nossiter's 1991 film, *Resident Alien*. And memorably there was his *Alternative Queen's Speech* delivered to the British nation from a horse drawn carriage in Central Park and broadcast by Channel 4 on Christmas Day, at exactly the same time as the real Queen's address – proof, if proof were needed, that by the end of his life he had truely become 'the stately homo of England'.

The more I looked at this material the more I realised that one of the major things Quentin had done in his life was mythologise his own past, turning his actual existence into an art form. I knew I had to disassemble these myths in order to try to make sense of him. I began to examine the stories which he had honed and developed over a lifetime, stories he had often shamelessly repeated from one book or interview to the next, to try to get below the surface of a man who always claimed he had no secrets and that 'what you saw was what you got'. Little did I know that, by the time my research was complete and the play was on the stage in London, Quentin would be dead and I would myself have become a character in the final chapters of that story, becoming embroiled in the fascinating, mysterious and, as yet, untold circumstances surrounding his death.

This book then is, in a way, the story of my research. It's the story of my attempts to get to the essence of an enigma, and to come to terms with what Quentin Crisp meant to me and to the age in which he lived. It's about how Denis Pratt, the self-confessed sissy from south Wimbledon ended up as Quentin Crisp, an iconic figure of the 20th century and the toast of New York. It's also about trying to make sense of why he ended his days in a boarding house, in a suburb of Manchester, in the heart of the country he had struggled for much of his adult life to escape from.

TOP: FROM LEFT TO RIGHT:
QUENTIN'S BROTHER, GERALD, HIS MOTHER,
'BABA', AND HIS FATHER, CHARLES SPENCER
BELOW: BABA IN LATER LIFE

The trouble with children

The trouble with children is they are not returnable.

Quentin Crisp, or Denis Pratt as he was christened, was born in Sutton, Surrey, on Christmas Day, 1908. By his own admission he was 'born to middle-class middling parents'. He said that the minute he stepped out of his mother's womb he realised that he had made a mistake and he 'shouldn't have come', but 'the trouble with children is they are not returnable'.

He was the youngest of four children. He had a brother of 13 months and another brother and sister of seven and eight, respectively. His father was a dour small-town lawyer who, it was said, put enough effort into the rounds of suburban tennis parties to secure a socially ambitious wife but who then promptly disappointed her by withdrawing from that world completely. Mr Crisp, senior, was a fastidious man who dusted the chairs on which the cat had been lying before occupying them, and who ate a banana with a knife and fork. From the accounts of Quentin's surviving relatives, such as his niece Frances Ramsay, and from his own recollections there was little emotional connection between the young Quentin and his father who, Quentin said, did not like him because his presence was 'insistently physical'. (From this, I think, we can safely infer that Quentin appeared a 'sissy' from a very early age.) However, he had a much stronger relationship with his mother who was much more lively and outgoing, with a love of people and storytelling. Whilst he would later portray his childhood as an endlessly suburban and rather tiresome experience, Frances recalls the family quite differently, saying all of them 'were eccentric in their own ways, but he was the only one to make a living from it'.

By the time Quentin came along the family were living in debt, which Quentin described as an improvement on poverty because it 'looked better'.

His parents, he remembers, were in a constant struggle to 'keep up with the Joneses' and it wasn't until he was older and got a place of his own that he realised how much cheaper it was 'to drag them down to your level', something he never tired of telling people.

As an infant Quentin contracted pneumonia, and was left with a taste for the attention that was heaped upon him as a consequence. 'Since an early age exhibitionism has been my drug, and I have taken doses of it so massive that they would have killed a normal person.' However, once he had recovered from his illness, his mother went back to apportioning her love equally between all her children, and he found he was no longer the star at the centre of his own universe. The young Quentin flew into 'an ungovernable rage' from which, he always maintained, he 'never fully recovered' because 'a fair share of anything is starvation diet to an ego maniac'.

His response to this 'unfairly equal' treatment at the hands of his mother was to invent an elaborate fantasy world for himself to inhabit. He would create characters to perform for the servants. He would rummage through the box rooms and the attics for his mother's old clothes and he would tour the house in her frocks. A wheelbarrow was his carriage, a tree branch his parasol and, as he did this, he would talk endlessly describing the splendours of the life he was living in his imagination. He could keep up these monologues for whole afternoons and, not surprisingly, the servants often took to spending extended periods dusting upstairs.

On one occasion his desire for attention led to an incident which clearly remained a vivid memory throughout his life. His nurse had told him and his brother that they were about to be taken for their usual walk and Quentin had begun to deploy his favourite delaying tactic of putting his arms rigidly at his side whilst she tried to put his coat on. Tired of these antics, she took his brother downstairs and they both hid. Not knowing they were doing this Quentin's mother, when he asked her where they had gone, told him he may go as far as the front gate to look for them. When Quentin got to the end of the path they were nowhere to be seen, so he continued on to the end of Brighton Road to look for them. Here he encountered what he called a 'rag and bone man', but his niece remembers as a 'gypsy', who offered him a lift on his cart. Not surprisingly his disappearance had caused a huge stir. His mother telephoned the police and the whole neighbourhood turned out to look for him. He was found a couple of hours later on Sutton Downs. The police took him to a doctor who examined him – and advised his mother never to question him about the incident. For many years Quentin said he was troubled by 'two half-formed memories'. In one of these memories the ground beneath him was covered in newspapers and when he put his hand underneath them he discovered something unpleasant, and in the other recollection he was drawing something long between his finger and thumb – 'a thin tube, a piece of cord' – and there were lumps inside the tube. Quentin later joked that this was his 'first instance of being picked up by a strange man on a street corner'. As usual Quentin turned a strange experience into a myth and an anecdote with a punch line. Nonetheless, this incident is very interesting as is the whole subject of abuse in relation to him. In *The Wit and Wisdom of Quentin Crisp*, compiled and edited by Guy Kettelhack in 1984, Quentin talks about another incident in which a man approached him when he was sitting alone on a park bench and inquired about the punishment of other boys at his school. The man wanted to know if the boys had their trousers pulled down before being smacked. Quentin said, to shut him up, he eventually told him they did just that. However, Kettelhack goes on to ask Quentin what he thinks about a child being sexually threatened by an adult, as Kettelhack put it, 'a child molester'. Quentin's answer is highly revealing. He says that one must distinguish between child molesters and people such as the man in the park, between those who actually commit 'physical acts' on the children and sodomise them, and those who 'merely tamper'. He says, 'You needn't worry about the psychological effects of most tampering; it's what's happening physically that counts.' He goes on to say, 'People are always trying to pretend that if you are tampered with by some person much older than yourself, your psyche is scarred for life, and I very much doubt this.' The psychological, he asserts, does not matter: 'Life in my opinion is entirely physical.'

His other early brush with sex came when a young actor 'who had played Bottom in more senses than one' came to direct a production of *A Midsummer*

Night's Dream at his brother's preparatory school. Quentin was allowed to take part wearing a 'wreath of roses and a green tulle dress'. He also got to sit on the knee of the said actor who, Quentin remembers, told him he was 'his favourite'. The same guy was arrested at Sutton train station the next day for molesting little boys. Quentin, of course, later said he was annoyed that he'd 'missed out on all the fun'.

At the halfway stage of the First World War, the family suffered what Quentin described as their 'first defeat at the hands of the Joneses', and were forced to move into a smaller house on the opposite side of the road. This provided the first major challenge for the young Quentin: not because of the financial implications of the move but because the family were forced to sacrifice their servants and so he lost his captive audience. Still, he refused to leave the world of his imagination, and was gradually reconciling himself to the fact that he preferred his fantasy life in which he was 'a woman, exotic and disdainful' to his real life in which he was merely a boy. One day he was invited to a nearby garden to play. In the garden a cousin of his playmate was present who suggested, to bring a little romance into their game, that she should stand on the veranda and watch jealously whilst Quentin, playing her lover, walked by with a friend on his arm. The young Quentin was instantly appalled at the prospect of playing the prince, and kicked up quite a fuss before his playmate quickly intervened saying that Quentin never played the role of a man. (He would later say that he wished he had been born a woman.) His mother seemed unconcerned with his obsessive female role play, and Quentin later speculated that this was because the lives he was acting out were secretly her own ideal. He said she allowed him at least to feel it was 'a taste they shared'.

During this time the bond between mother and son grew stronger and she encouraged him to stretch his imagination in a number of ways. She took him to his first grown-up entertainment, a play called *Chu Chin Chow*, with a character called Miss Hayworth who apparently had 'saucers on her breasts' and 'a dirty clothes basket on her head' and walked up and down stairs with her hands at 'the utmost of horizontal positions'. The young Quentin nearly fainted with delight. She also introduced him to Lord Leighton's classical mock-ups and to the world of literature: before bed *The Lady Of The Lake* and the *Idylls Of The King* were read to him in her best poetry voice, and when she was exhausted she handed him fairy tales to read for himself. This he did with great relish. She couldn't have known it but his mother was arming him with the crucial weapon he would later use to defend himself against a hostile world. However, all that would come much later. First there were the horrors of school to face.

FROM LEFT TO RIGHT:
SIBLINGS GERALD, LEWIS AND PHYLLIS

I learned nothing at school

I learned nothing at school except how to bare injustice.

Whilst at home Quentin said he managed to make his life miserable 'more or less unaided', at preparatory school this was done for him. The teachers picked on him because he was an easy target and the rest of the school laughed at him with his 'unfortunate teeth' and awkward physicality. He regularly arrived at the school gates awash with tears and caked in excrement, unwilling to pull away from his mother, which of course prompted even more ridicule.

At preparatory school he won a very poor scholarship to a minor public school on the borders of Staffordshire and Derbyshire that looked like 'a cross between a prison and a church', where he said he learned nothing 'except how to bare injustice'. This, however, was crucial to his development. Before going there his mother warned him not to repeat the mistake of arriving at the school gates in tears and not to respond to other boys when they bullied him, as this only encouraged them further. It seems he took her advice to heart and he somehow managed to grow the extra layer of skin (or two) that would remain with him throughout his life.

Another crucial discovery, that came at boarding school, was that he was attracted to other boys. It was a public school – he was not alone. The major relationships were between older and younger boys and the sex lives of the prefects fascinated the youngsters, Quentin included. Unfortunately, when this fascination spread to open contact it often ended in tears, with the younger boys dragged in front of the whole school and caned for climbing drainpipes, Romeo and Juliet style, to get into the dorms of the prefects. The draconian attitude of the headmaster, Quentin's own lack of attractiveness, 'my hair was rich brown and straight but unfortunately my teeth were not', and his desire 'to use sex as a weapon to allure, subjugate and if possible destroy the personality of others', meant he made no inroads with his contemporaries. Quentin said he longed to be the subject of a school-shaking romance but relationships in which personality was not involved were, he said, 'valueless to him'. Perhaps, as a result, he became more interested in the masters. He said he tried to seduce them all the time. His means of doing this was to work incredibly hard at his lessons and be keen to take exams. At these he shined, not because of any great knowledge but because of an incredible memory. 'I used to go into the examination room with pale lips mumbling whole vocabularies of Latin military words and come out again thoroughly relaxed knowing nothing.' This ability to remember huge chunks of text would later become his ticket into 'the public speaking racket' when he learned almost verbatim huge sections of his own book *How To Have A Life-Style* for a performance at the King's Head theatre in London. However, at this stage in his life, his impressive memory only served to make him look a swot and this, in turn, further alienated him from the other boys. To the end of his life he had a mark on his arm where his 'friends' had attempted to saw through his wrist with a jagged ruler.

This lack of success with other boys and failure to woo the masters, who were now equally alienated by his smartness, led Quentin to discover what he described as the only fact of life he claimed he ever really understood.

> *Masturbation is not only an expression of self-regard: it is also the natural emotional outlet of those who, before anything has reared its ugly head, have already accepted as inevitable the wide gulf between their real futures and expectations of their fantasies.*

The habit fitted neatly into his well-established world of make-believe and became lifelong.

> *In an incorrigible fantasist masturbation soon ceases to be what it is for other people, an admitted substitute for intercourse. It is sexual intercourse that becomes a substitute – and a poor one – for masturbation. … Universal love goes with masturbation.*

Interestingly many years later when Jack Gold would come to turn *The Naked Civil Servant* into a TV film it would be the masturbation scene in the bath that he would have most trouble getting past the TV bosses. So much so that, in the end, the caption below the scene read, 'Isn't bath time fun?' Only later would the real caption be restored.

However, perhaps the major discovery Quentin made at boarding school was a method of dealing with what he called 'his greatest gift: unpopularity'. Whilst at preparatory school this gulf between him and his contemporaries prompted despair and tears, and any number of attempts to change his image; now it prompted something quite different. Instead of attempting to be different he discovered the virtue in becoming more like himself, in actually playing the role that others had cast him in. If people laughed at his physical awkwardness, he would exaggerate it further; if his speech amused, he would make it more extreme. 'I learned to consciously achieve an effect that originally I had produced by accident.' He would later assert that,

> *The time comes for everybody when he has to do deliberately what he used to do by mistake, it is the only way you can get the joke on your own terms. I made it clear I knew what it was they were laughing at and this made my life much easier to bare. It lessened the tension between me and other people and this is in my view the beginning of your own style. ... The great trick with life is not to become like other people but to become more like yourself.*

Already the young Quentin was practising the habits that would later become a philosophy. He was also beginning the retreat into the 'strong, sad, kingdom of self'.

The life of a homosexual

The life of a homosexual is so horrible. It's not the social persecution, it's what you are expected to do.

By the time Quentin reached 18 he had lost all interest in study (though at some expense as his father had dispatched him to London University on a journalism course) and he was beginning to think that sexually he was 'quite unlike anyone else in the world'. His father despaired of him and the gulf between the two of them was widening, Quentin himself had absolutely no inkling of where he may get work or to where his life was leading until a chance encounter with an eccentric friend of a friend of his mother's.

Mrs Longhurst was a 'big striding, strident woman of about 40'. She was a stewardess and sometime portrait model who lived in Charlotte Street in a flat with walls covered in African knives. After an initial encounter Quentin became a regular visitor to her strange West End abode where the two would play long games of pontoon and talk. She spoke in a wildly exaggerated manner and often epigrammatically. 'Don't live in Hampstead,' she told him. 'That's where the parents lived and they were crippled with rheumatism – bed ridden. They moved and what happened? Within a week they were dancing in the streets of Maida Vale.' She was Quentin's first brush with Bohemia, the first person he had encountered who 'did not fly to extremes' but 'lived there', and he loved it. Also, crucially, he learned to ape her exaggerated mode of speech. He said he 'practised it', until eventually it became his own.

Quentin said Mrs Longhurst's attitude to homosexuality was 'the same as it was to most things; she treated the subject with mocking curiosity'. However, she was not hostile or, at least, nothing like as hostile as the rest of the world Quentin encountered. He said Britain was

*... still stumbling around in search of a weapon with which to exterminate the
monster whose shape and size were not yet known or even guessed at, but that was
thought to be Greek in origin, smaller than socialism, but more deadly –
especially to children.*

Quentin said he never recalled hearing anyone talk about the subject then,
except Mrs Longhurst who, interestingly, he heard discuss it with his mother.
Soon afterwards he began to broach the subject himself with his mother who,
it seems, had some notion of what Quentin was really saying. However his
father remained 'invincibly ignorant', and was much more concerned with
Quentin's academic failure.

When he left King's College in London, it was without the diploma in
journalism he had gone there to take. That said, he had at least been
introduced to the principles of it, and it was a skill that would be very useful
in later life. Quentin was always acutely aware of what was necessary to say
and do in order to get on the front pages of the newspapers.

After ending the course it seems he spent 'many months' idling at home,
getting on his parents' nerves. He became so listless that his mother thought
that he was ill and sent him to the doctor who, without making any
examination, said all he needed was a 'lesson in life'. Shortly afterwards, whilst
wandering the streets of the West End, he stumbled on the truth that the
doctor had ordered: he discovered he was not alone.

There, on Shaftesbury Avenue and Piccadilly, he discovered young men
standing in doorways making comments like, ' Isn't it terrible tonight, dear?
No men about. The 'dilly's not what it used to be.' Though Quentin said that
an Indian boy at his school had once 'amazed everyone with the story of his
encounter with male prostitutes in Birmingham', Quentin had never dreamed
he would actually meet one. There they were on the streets of London; there
for all to see. Soon afterwards he discovered a café in Soho called the Black
Cat which was frequented by other homosexuals. Of course, in those days
there was no such thing as a designated 'gay café', but here the owner at least
tolerated Quentin and his kind, and Quentin said he took to spending 'day

after uneventful day, night after loveless night' with the boys, 'buying each other cups of tea, combing each other's hair and trying on each other's lipsticks'. He said the danger in which they all lived 'bound them together' and though there was a lot of 'stylised cattiness' none of it was ever 'unkindly meant'. Whilst it is hard to imagine this was entirely true and perhaps, with time, Quentin had rather sentimentalised his introduction to the Black Cat, clearly here amongst the camp male prostitutes and assorted outsiders, or 'hooligans' as he loved to call them, he discovered a new 'family'. He said they would spend hours 'fingering over the great figures of history and identifying which of them were or could possibly have been gay'. At this stage Oscar Wilde was their greatest hero: a man who 'threw away his life for the man he loved' was how Quentin described people's way of representing him. If Quentin ever subscribed to this opinion he would severely revise it in later life saying to me in our last meeting:

> *Nothing could be further from the truth. When Mr Wilde came out of gaol (and he'd only been there two years) he fell apart completely and spent the rest of his life in a drunken stupor in Paris. I've known people who were in prison twice as long without writing any of that bad verse, and when they came out of jail they went on with their lives, shaken, but they went on with their lives. But Mr Wilde must have accepted the judgment passed on him by society or else he would not have been crushed by it. One is left dazed by the discrepancy between the way he saw himself and the way anyone else would have seen him. First of all there was no need for him to bring a case against Mr Queensberry. Secondly he could have evaded the case and was advised to do so by his friends and when in court with the case going against him he continued pert replies and thirdly he dragged the fair name of Mr Plato into this sordid case. He was mentioning 'the love that dare not speak it's name'. How can love be used in a case where the names of dozens of young men had been read out that Mr Wilde only met in braille? Procured for him by Lord Alfred Douglas and devoured behind closed curtains in a darkened room. He had no idea of just how sordid his life seemed to the rest of the world, he lived in a dream.*

When he told me this story, and he had clearly told it a thousand times, he did so with real, not manufactured, anger. There was something about Wilde that got right under Quentin's skin. Perhaps this additional comment explains it.

> *As I see it when he was in prison it was his style that was destroyed, which proves it was never really a part of him but a sequined Band-Aid covering a suppurating sore of self-hatred.*

Now there are many who saw in Quentin a huge well of self-loathing: despite all he said, he could still declare that homosexuality was an 'abnormality that he wouldn't wish on anyone'. Is it possible that the reason he hated Wilde was not, as he asserted, that his life was 'sordid' and that he gave pert replies in court, but that he saw in Wilde something of himself; or was it merely that people always wanted to see Quentin as the natural successor to Wilde and he wanted to distance himself and become his own man?

However, whilst he may not have agreed with his friends about Mr Wilde, he still learned a huge amount in 'The Cat'. As he came to understand the lives of other homosexuals he began to understand his own. He had begun his journey to 'the interior', as he loved to call it. Quentin said he

> *... soon learned by heart every argument that could be reared in the climate of the time against the persecution of homosexuals: we weren't doing any harm, we couldn't help it and though this was hardly watertight from a legal point of view – we had enough to bare already.*

He also discovered that, in this world, romance was quite different from the fiction he had read in his youth. He began to accept money for sex: 'After all a ten-shilling note shows incontrovertibly just how mad about you a man is.' Apart from needing the money (he was still living at home on pocket money) he said it 'absolved him of the duty of enjoying sex for its own sake'. As a result, he said, courtship consisted of

> *... walking down a street with a man who held my arm in a merciless grip until we came to a dark doorway whereupon he said, 'This'll do.' The venality of my predicament I took calmly. Unlike Desdemona, I could perform the deed but not say the word.*

It is difficult to say for how long Quentin was a prostitute. My own suspicion, from talking to him, is that it didn't last as long as many people assume and that often in retelling the story he blurs the distinction between prostitution and unsatisfactory casual sex in shop doorways with strange men. Whatever the truth of it, the essence was the same – yet more disappointment in the sexual department.

Despite this wild introduction to the world of Soho, his outlook was still so limited that he assumed all 'deviates were openly despised and rejected'. To begin with he enjoyed this aspect. He said that 'their grief and fear' drew his 'melancholy nature very strongly'. 'At first I only wanted to wallow in their misery but as time went by, I longed to reach its very essence until finally I desired to represent it.' By this process Quentin would eventually play a significant part in shifting homosexuality from being a 'burden to a cause'. But that would come much later. First there was the challenge of taking his battle beyond the confines of London W1.

London was relatively easy

London was relatively easy, the rest of the country was straightforward missionary territory.

By the time he was 23, Quentin Crisp had decided it was no good being homosexual in the West End where 'sin reigned supreme' or in Soho which was inhabited by 'outcasts of all kinds'. He wanted to carry out an 'assault on the rest of England' which he saw as 'straightforward missionary country'. Whilst his voice and his physical manner had always given him away as different, he felt that these had often been written off by others as something he 'couldn't help'. What he now wanted to do was to make certain people knew he was doing it because he wanted to, and so he started to display symptoms which 'could not be thought accidental' – he began to wear make-up and openly effeminate and outrageous clothes. He began to go about his daily life looking 'undeniably homosexual'.

Despite the fact that he had grown used to being picked upon at school nothing could have prepared him for the response he got in the streets of thirties' London. Total strangers would slap his face on tube platforms and gangs of lads would pull him into shop doorways and give him a good hiding on the way home. He learned the routes which took him away from the main streets, often walking miles out of his way in the process. But he refused to compromise his look, after years of playing on the back foot he was taking the game to the opposition.

At home the story was quite different, and he kept his new appearance and life away from his parents, choosing to don his 'war paint' in a nearby public lavatory after leaving home and keeping his two worlds quite separate. Not that his mother was entirely ignorant and one day she questioned him as to the reason he never brought any of his new friends home. Quentin told her that she 'would hate them, if he did'. She accepted this and an uneasy truce was broached between them which would endure throughout their lives. No such truce was established with his father though, and it didn't take long for any conversation between the two to stray into his father inquiring, less than politely, when he was going to sort out his life and get a career. At the end of one such chat his father said, 'The trouble with you is you look like a male whore.' This comment Quentin remembered as a turning point. It could have crushed him, but instead it had quite the opposite effect. It liberated him. He accepted without argument what his father said and, at a stroke, released himself from 'the never-land between sin and virtue' and took his 'final vows'. He told his father that at Christmas, when he next went to London, he may not come back. He was true to his word.

Back in the land of shop-doorway queens and delicious sin, Quentin said the 'the world lay all before him, like a 'trap-door' and he wandered aimlessly amongst the bright lights of Shaftesbury Avenue and Piccadilly Circus in search of a future. Just when it appeared that no such prospect existed he had an encounter with a boy he had first met in the Black Cat. 'This boy had caused quite a stir by boasting to the habitués that he wasn't on the game.' As proof of this claim Quentin said he 'had often carried books under his arm and snubbed the other members of the clientele with snippets of literature – chiefly by Michael Arlen'. Quentin said, 'He was the least likable of the lot. It was inevitable that I got to know him best.' This boy was one of the few regulars of 'The Cat' who lived alone, and he invited Quentin to share a room with him in Barons Court. This lasted three months during which sex, according to Quentin, was 'never on the menu'. The two were broke and managed to feed themselves by perpetrating an elaborate scam on the Lyons Corner House chain which avoided paying the bill and meant that, as long as they visited a different branch every day, they could live on relatively little. The scam involved one of them leaving the restaurant when the meal was complete whilst the other visited the lavatory. On the way back from the lavatory, if apprehended, the person would say the other had paid. If this was accepted all was fine, if not he would pay the bill saying he thought his friend had paid. Providing they had the money for the meal in their pockets it was almost impossible for them to be actually accused of a real criminal act.

The rest of their time was spent hanging around the streets of Soho 'in search of love, or money, or both' and, back at home in the cramped Barons Court flat, Quentin would quote extensively from the plays and novels he had begun to write. These were often historical in nature and, as Quentin would later say, 'turgid in the extreme'.

During this time in Barons Court Quentin's father lost his 'great gamble with the future' and died. Quentin said that when the telegram announcing his father's death arrived, he felt 'nothing except irritation at having to go back home'. His great fear was that when he returned he would be tempted to stay and, however difficult his new life was in London, he knew it was what he must do. And he did: after the funeral he returned to London.

Despite the fact that his friendship with the Barons Court boy was by now based on 'mutual nagging and antipathy', on his return the two of them moved into another flat, this time in Kings Cross. Shortly afterwards, at his friend's behest, Quentin ventured onto the stage to support a dancer's attempt at a publicity grabbing record of 32 fouettés. The record attempt failed, and Quentin's supporting appearance was almost as big a let-down. All the same, it was an early taste of the life to come – a life that in thirties' London he still could not even imagine.

When I say you must lie alone

When I say you must lie alone I am not trying to curtail your sex lives. I am merely trying to snatch the straw from your beak and prevent all this nesting.

After his father's death, Quentin's mother had even more time on her hands to try and fix Quentin up with a 'life', and she arranged for him, via another friend of a friend, to be employed by a firm of consulting electrical engineers. A less suitable arena it is hard to imagine. However, this new 'career' enabled Quentin to leave his Barons Court buddy (their relationship had now declined to one of open hostility – 'an old married couple minus the sex') and to move into a flat of his own. On arriving there, he said that he felt the thrill he had heard others talk of when they had moved into a house with a partner.

The heightened sense of the world around them, the inability to refrain from taking little skips as they walked – all these were mine on realising that I might with luck never have to live with anyone again.

He never did – and another stage on the 'journey to the interior' was complete.

The room he took was in 'darkest Pimlico', in those days a far cry from its present upmarket status. The room had 'Nottingham lace curtains at the windows, corned-beef linoleum on the floor and a brass bedstead in one corner'. His friends inquired when he was going to 'chi-chi it up'. He told them he wasn't; he was happy. Again he was true to his word, and so began another lifelong habit – seeming obliviousness to the creature comforts many people crave. Save for a brief sojourn at The Chelsea Hotel when he arrived in New York, he would live the rest of his adult life in one-room bedsits. 'What is the use of having a home with two rooms?' he asked me on my visit. 'What do you do with the other room when you are not in it?' This lack of interest in the size of his home was mirrored by an equal indifference to the decoration and maintenance within it. He seldom cooked and he never cleaned. 'After the first four years the dust doesn't get any worse. It's just a question of not losing your nerve.' He never did.

Whilst the fruits of his new career pleased him, the career itself was, not surprisingly, less of a success. He was employed as an engineer's tracer, a job he said he could never hope to become proficient at because accuracy was 'alien' to his nature – something of a problem in a job in which accuracy was its very *raison d'être*. When he was given plans to trace he 'copied the mistakes as well as the revisions and neither of them properly', and when he was told to transfer the electric pylons from one map to another he did so with such 'abandon' that he would joke later that there were probably many women and clergymen reading his books who 'had electricity pylons in their roses and poking out of the top of their church steeples'. When he was not blighting the English countryside with his copying skills, he worked further at his plays, poems and libretti. All of which, he said, contained ideas which were far too highbrow for his 'sub-Tennysonian' style. Though he was getting far closer to knowing who he was as a man, he had still a long way to go in his journey to find his identity as a writer.

During this time he began another habit that was to become lifelong. He assembled around him a group of friends on the fringes of society. There was a male prostitute named Greta ('on account of his love for Miss Garbo'), a female student from High Wycombe who he said threw herself at his feet saying she wasn't worthy of him, a model he met in Hyde Park who brought with him a Czech gentleman with 'an unspellable name', and an Irishman with his friend who constantly borrowed money. This pleased Quentin greatly because it was a novelty to know someone who was actually poorer than himself. He would later say to me, 'If you have love to give you must give it to the unlovable, anything else would be unfair.' And throughout his adult life Quentin remained a magnet for, and a beacon to, the outsiders of society.

Meantime his appearance had now progressed from the 'effeminate to the downright bizarre' and the reaction he got in the streets had progressed to even more open hostility. Many was the time the police would have to be brought in to move on 'spectators watching the baying mob' as they taunted him. Quentin said that he was 'excited, exhausted and worried by them but not frightened, because he still believed he could educate them'.

Not surprisingly, deep down, he was still not happy. However, far from placing the blame at the feet of an intolerant world, he laid the fault firmly at his own door: he was spending too much time living in the future, dreaming of publishing his Helen of Troy play and of becoming a success rather than living the life that was delivered to him.

> *The essence of happiness is its absoluteness. It is automatically the state of being of those who live in the continuous present all over their bodies. No effort is required to define or even attain happiness but enormous concentration is needed to abandon everything else.*

This was a skill that would later become a central part of his philosophy and an abiding theme in his books. He would often talk of his ability, learned in childhood, to do nothing save for lying on his bed breathing and blinking. It was again a trick that would serve him well when he became an artist's model.

He was learning to take responsibility for his own life and beginning to fully understand that his life was not just what happened to him, but how he responded to it.

The obviously queer boys

The obviously queer boys were spoiling it for the rest.

Not surprisingly the job at the electrical contractors didn't last and, when the extent of his failure to accurately copy the positions of electricity pylons became clear, he was promptly sacked. This threw him 'head first into insolvency' and introduced him to the Pentonville Labour Exchange where he quickly became a 'figure of derision' and, were it not for the kindness of a sympathetic manager, he may have come to rest as an unknown, eccentric, failed commercial artist. This manager took him on one side and politely suggested that, looking as he did, he was rather less than likely to be a front runner for other jobs as a commercial artist and perhaps should consider a change of career. Yet again Quentin maintains in retelling this story that the decision was taken for him, by someone else. He always liked to say he merely did what others told him and to some extent this was true. However, whilst he had been at the contractors, Quentin had embarked on an evening course in life drawing and illustration at Regent Street Polytechnic – the Principal of St Martins School Of Art had turned him down saying 'it was a miracle he had any job at all and had better not try to change it' – and the manager immediately agreed that he was more likely to find work in a studio than in an office. After a brief sojourn in a publisher's office (another job arranged by his mother who was by now digging right down to the core of her social strata) he managed to secure a job in one of the new and trendy studios that had sprung up in Fleet Street and Chancery Lane. There he learned something of the trade of advertising, a trade that in those days he said was thought of in much the same way as burglary. This didn't last long and after a number of dismissals from similar establishments, an act which 'invariably prompted a mixture of indignation and relief', he stumbled upon a way of preventing it happening again: he gave up work. He was 28. From this point on Quentin claims he never did anything for long if he didn't want to

– except grow old. (This assertion would come back to haunt him in his last days on earth.)

Meantime, prosperity was gradually returning to England and the nation was in one of its 'periodic re-evaluations of the spectre of homosexuality'. He said that 'previously it was thought to be an affliction which only affected ballet dancers and actors' but, suddenly, 'people were worrying that it was beginning to knock at the door of ordinary, decent citizens'. As a consequence, the police began one of their spasmodic 'clean ups' of the West End. When he was younger, Quentin noted, a policeman who had apprehended him on a street corner had just warned him in a fatherly tone, seemingly believing that the only men who would sleep with Quentin were those suffering from venereal disease who women wouldn't go near. Now the mood was very different, and the police started to use decoys as a means to round up the buggers. This tactic was mainly deployed in public lavatories, but also in the shop doorways of Piccadilly. Alongside this, they stepped up their raids on the clubs where men met, imprisoning those in charge of them for months on end. Amongst them was a friend of Quentin's.

As a result of this purge a number of the bars and clubs which Quentin had previously frequented began to reject him, as did a number of other homosexuals. He simply looked too queer and people did not want to risk being associated with a man who flaunted his difference so outrageously. Quentin felt this rejection much more acutely than that by the straight society who he had taken pleasure in annoying and in trying to educate as to his plight. To be rejected by his own kind left a deep wound that he would never forget. An American actor said to him that 'obviously queer boys were spoiling it for the rest'. It was a comment, the essence of which would be repeated to him in differing contexts throughout his whole life.

As a result of this rejection, Quentin turned for friendship to the straight world whose 'tolerance he put to the test, not by the risk of involving them in a scandal but by never talking for long about anything but the social problems of his kind'. Amongst those who began to carry this burden was the wife of his Czech friend with the 'unspellable name'. She was an artist's model, 'dressed in accordance with the rigid dress laws of the time'. Quentin said, 'Her days were spent working in art schools and her evenings were spent complaining of her husband who in her absence pawned her gramophone.' They were a lively pair and introduced a continental flavour into Quentin's life with their endless talk of sex and their strange diet of sea wrack and stew. 'Mrs Czech', as Quentin always called her, thought of homosexuality as nothing more than 'a minor, curious fact of life', and this disturbed his essential puritanism. Up to this point in his life he said that 'every opportunity for pleasure had carried with it an almost equally strong desire to do without'. But he saw in the Czech couple the possibility of 'unfettered pleasure'; he also saw the downside when, one evening, he went into the kitchen and discovered Mr Czech in a passionate embrace with one of Quentin's male friends from art school. For the first time Quentin was forced to 'admit that other people existed, it was not a discovery I welcomed'. Significantly though, he was forced to break out of the gay ghetto that he had been so happy to temporarily immerse himself in.

Sex is the last refuge of the miserable

Sex is the last refuge of the miserable. Does anyone really want to put someone's penis in their mouth? It's so disgusting I couldn't bare it.

The rest of the thirties were spent in much the same way as they had begun. Quentin moved from room to room, and from freelance job to freelance job. He would often stay as the guest of friends in rooms - that he said they couldn't hope to let 'to any normal person'; and he always claimed he went wherever he was asked to go rather than actually making any real decisions for himself. His friends continued to be people on the fringes of contemporary society. He was to an extent living the bohemian life of characters potrayed in Rodney Ackland's plays like *Absolute Hell*. There was surface glitter and underlying poverty; and still no clear sense of where he was going.

Periodic forays into the world of sexual encounters invariably, if he is to be believed, ended in disaster. There was a much recounted trip to the, then, gay Mecca of England, Portsmouth, where he pursued the goal of bedding a man in uniform; but only succeeded in picking up a couple of middle-aged ex-seamen with pot bellies and spending the evening in a homeless canteen after being locked out of his guest house. Interestingly though, when the film of *The Naked Civil Servant* was made, this became a fantasy sequence in which Quentin was surrounded by beautiful sailors in crisp white uniforms. It was a sequence that would live in popular consciousness for the next 25 years, so much so that in the year 2000, when the public voted on their all time top-100 television moments, it was included. The TV critic David Aaronivitch said it was the first time he recalled seeing a positive image of homosexuality on TV. The reality of that journey to Portsmouth for Quentin, however, had been very different. He was fast coming to the conclusion that the kind of sex life other people spoke about was to remain, for him, a distant island. But, he had yet to accept this and turn this fact to his advantage. And before he could do so, war broke out.

On hearing the news Quentin said he went out and bought two pounds of henna and made up his mind to 'ignore the War completely', refusing to listen to the wireless or buy newspapers, 'receiving news of Mr Hitler's advance into Poland only from a friend, long after the event'. It was a tactic he would go on to deploy in many contexts. 'If I am unhappy I tell myself I am not unhappy and after a while I cease to be unhappy.' In today's therapy culture it would be classed as mere denial but, for Quentin, it seemed to be about something else. He claimed to be capable of living in the present and blocking out all that he did not wish to connect with. For a man who argued that he avoided decisions this was yet another curious contradiction.

War had a dramatic effect on the economy and most of his freelance work dried up. This compelled him to change address on a number of occasions in search of ever-cheaper rooms: he sank socially from Belgravia to Fulham and then, later, to Chelsea. When he moved there, to Beaufort Street, he was offered furniture by a friend of his who was an ex-ballet teacher. Somehow Quentin never got around to arranging for it to be moved and, as a result, he arrived at the tiny unfurnished room without possessions. This he recalled as 'a stroke of enormous good fortune', for he discovered that the unfurnished life was very much to his liking. Somehow he felt free, it was as if he was finally beginning to shake off his socially aspirant background. For the first time he truly had life on his own terms. He decided he would never 'become a thrall to the rituals of domesticity'. Quentin had seen his mother's life become engulfed by such activity. He vividly remembered sitting on the floor watching her take every single one of the works of Bulwer-Lytton down from the shelf to dust them. He had said, 'I shouldn't do all that.' She replied, 'I know you wouldn't. That's why I must.' If only she had known. From here on in Quentin would never live in what he called 'the captivity of hygiene'. He never cleaned and he never made the bed and he took to spending huge amounts of time lying on his back 'pretending he was in his coffin'. He said he slipped from his bed in the morning 'like a letter from an envelope' and,

... save for the thickening film of sullied cold cream that as time went by piled up

on the pillow-slip, no-one would have been able to detect that my bed had been occupied.

The only problem he discovered with this new life was the dust he accumulated on his trousers whilst putting them on – however he soon found a remedy and proceeded to jump in the air whilst performing the task, or so he said ...

This room was to be his home for another 30 years until he left for the bright lights of America and, though he couldn't have known it, part of his passage to fame as it would feature as the setting for Denis Mitchell's *World In Action* documentary about him. It was also intriguingly to be the inspiration for Harold Pinter's first play, *The Room*, written after the then relatively unknown Pinter had paid Quentin a visit.

An actor's kingdom is divided

An actor's kingdom is divided into three provinces – the dressing room, the rehearsal room and the stage. Everything else is unreal.

As more and more dust fell on the early-Caledonian furnishings of his room, Quentin waited for his call-up papers. While other districts of London were busy fire-watching and digging trenches the inhabitants of the Kings Road were, to Quentin's eyes, mainly occupied with amateur theatricals in which he too became involved through a Miss Murison who had asked Quentin to write a review for her company. Unfortunately, by the time he had finished it, she and her co-directors had already embarked upon a production of *The Scarlet Pimpernel* instead. Quentin said,

> *The production was staged in a theatre so small that the leading lady was unable to enter the stage in her hat and was forced to hold down the brim like it was a pair of ear muffs. The stage was the size of a kitchen table though not so strongly constructed.*

This ill-advised production was followed by a work called *Fishing For Shadows*. Such was the level of preparation that went into this that Acts Two and Three were still being translated as Act One was being rehearsed. Miss Murison had asked the translator to find a play which would 'take people's minds off the horrors of war'. Unfortunately, by the time the translation was complete, Quentin said she realised that 'almost every scene contained a suicide'. Miss Murison said, 'You promised me a comedy.' To which her young translator replied, 'It's as funny as *The Seagull.'*

Undeterred by all of this Quentin wrote another piece. He called it an 'anti-Pirandello play' but it was never staged. This diversion of amateur theatricals was upstaged, anyway, by the arrival of his call-up papers. It was the first April of the War and Quentin was required to put in an appearance before the medical board. He set out for the Drill Hall in Kingston.

The minute he stood before the first doctor, he said, 'Harley Street collapsed'. He wore no make-up, his hair was down to his shoulders and was crimson from seven years of being hennaed, and his eyebrows were no longer straight making it obvious they had been plucked. Not surprisingly these, and other manifestations of effeminacy, disturbed the board deeply. Even whilst he was having his eyes tested he was told: 'You've dyed your hair. This is a sign of sexual perversion, do you know what I mean?' Quentin told him he did and that he was homosexual. 'The doctor practically collapsed and crawled from the room to consult with a colleague.'

After the fuss caused by his hair, attention switched to his anus. Quentin said his inquisitor's 'private dreams of the lives of homosexuals must have been very lurid indeed'. When he was vertical once again another man entered the room carrying a sheaf of paper: Quentin would never be required due to 'suffering from sexual perversion'.

This story would later become a favourite Kings Road anecdote and, on telling to a friend of his, he received the response 'suffering from, don't you mean glorying in?' It was typical of Quentin to turn what must have been one of the most humiliating experiences of his life into a story he could use to amuse people. It was a form of revenge on the forces repressing him – it still hurt though and this, combined with the effect war was having on his ability to get work, brought Quentin to his lowest point. With no job and with little prospect of a future that he could embrace, he felt destined to be permanently an outcast. He hadn't even enough money to buy his evening meal. He considered suicide but never attempted it, he said, because he was afraid.

A lifetime of never making positive decisions, accepting instead the least of the evils presented to me, had atrophied my will. It was not so much that I longed for death but that I didn't long for life. Hopelessness was thinly spread like drizzle over my whole outlook. But in an emergency I could not find a puddle of despondency deep enough to drown in.

However just when it appeared that the War was going to break, Quentin on the rocks of destitution, his 'window on the world' (as he called his telephone) came to the rescue. The phone was a recent acquisition and was a hugely significant step in his life. Through this device Quentin discovered a whole new world. It suddenly meant, he said, that even when there was no-one to chat to on the Kings Road he could 'chat to people deep in suburbia'. It was also a means of attracting more freelance work from people he had not yet met. Quentin said,

> [A] pessimist is someone who, if he is in the bath will not get out to answer the phone. I was incorrigibly hopeful. I never willingly let the bell ring for fear I might miss a message from God. I used to answer the phone with the words 'Yes, Lord'.

On this occasion the caller was of this world, a complete stranger who Quentin called Mr Hall, who asked him if he could paint his portrait. Quentin was quite taken aback but quickly regained his composure to enquire if he would be paid for the activity. Mr Hall said, 'Only if it's absolutely necessary.' Quentin said it was; and proceeded to take down the address of his studio. When he arrived there he said he

> ... recognised Mr Hall as one of the landmarks of the area, a man he had often seen in the Kings Road wearing a huge black hat and a pointed beard with which it would have been possible to scrub the sink.

Quentin was delighted. This was the first real artist's studio he had been in and Mr Hall was the first real artist he had ever met. Quentin loved the fact that he looked so perfectly the part and was fascinated by his first glimpse of an artist's inner sanctum.

Quentin said that his friends were 'deeply suspicious and thought that Mr Hall's intentions may be less than honourable'. They were wrong; and Quentin's portrait ended up in the Burlington Galleries. Sadly, by the time it appeared, the financial gain he had made from the project had long since disappeared. However his other gain was to be more enduring. Though he never established any kind of close bond with the man, he was flattered by his charm and courtesy and by the fact that he 'lacked the brutish iconoclasm with which many sought to establish themselves as 'characters'. Quentin had met a role model and the traits he admired in the painter would later become ones by which Quentin Crisp himself would become known – no matter how outrageous his comments, they were always delivered with the most impeccable manners and profound charm. It had also given him his first taste of a job that would provide his income for the next 20 years and, ultimately, give him the inspiration for the title of the book that would lift him out of obscurity. He became a professional poser – an artist's model.

What have you got against the wall?

When people ask me what I've got against art, I ask them 'What have you got against the wall?'

As with much else in Quentin's life this career change came more as a result of fate than intention. He was called up by a friend he had known when he first lived in Chelsea. She was a professional life model who was unable to keep an engagement in the Toynbee Hall, and she implored Quentin to take her place. 'You're always saying it must be nice to be a model. Now's your chance.' Unable to muster a 'no': Quentin reluctantly said 'yes'.

Having been an art student himself he knew that, unlike on the continent, English art school models were not entirely naked in front of female students and so, as soon as the receiver was back in it's place, Quentin said he went to work on a pair of old underpants with some shears. He cut away at everything except the waistband and a small patch of material in the front. He was ready for his new job.

The following evening he arrived in Toynbee Hall for a four-hour evening class. The master asked him to stand with the top of the screen behind him in a sort of crucifixion pose. Quentin duly obliged and when at ten o'clock he found himself still conscious he knew that he had finally found another way of earning a living. Moreover, to some extent he thought it to be the perfect job. 'It was easy to do, required no aptitude, no education, no references and no previous experience.' Allied to this was the fact that war was still raging and Quentin was one of the few male persons left in civilian life 'with two arms and two legs'. He applied to the secretaries of many of the London schools and a few immediately gave him work. However, most of his trade came from the suburban schools where his exoticism proved a bonus.

Posing was the first job he had had that he said he 'fully understood'. Up until this point he had always worked, or tried to work, to a standard other than his own. In commercial art, he said, he had always made an effort to draw things so that others would find them appetising and worth their money; and in his writing he had attempted to describe ideas so that others found them interesting. He decided to set about modelling in the opposite way – to force upon the students the qualities that he felt life drawing ought to possess. He was a success.

Although on one such mission he did almost come to grief. It was the day before the Easter holiday and he was standing in the corridor of a large technical college outside London waiting for his wages, when a student who he had previously only exchanged a few polite words with came up and, without any prompting, took his hand and kissed it before running away. A week or two later the girl wrote to him, asking if they could meet. Foolishly, thinking her request entirely innocent, Quentin invited her to London and introduced her to a number of his friends in 'the hooligan cafés of West London'. However just before she left, while they were standing in Holborn waiting for her bus, she suddenly threw herself at Quentin bringing him to the ground and imploring him to kiss her. A week later another letter arrived, this time from one of the girl's friends, saying she was suicidal and might do something silly if Quentin refused to meet her again. He replied telling her that he was homosexual. She wrote back in more grief and this went on for some time until she finally gave up on him. Afterwards one of Quentin's friends asked him how he could have been so naive as to have believed she merely wanted to be his soulmate. He replied that his sin was 'not *naïveté* but vanity'. He said he had always been, and still remained, reluctant to forego a single ounce of friendship and had imagined that he could somehow fashion the girl's attitude to him into something merely platonic. Again, it was a trait that would remain with him throughout his life and it meant that, no matter how famous he became, his name was never removed from the phone book and he would gladly meet for lunch anyone who called him up. The word he claimed he found the hardest to say in the English language was 'no'.

It was in the world of night-school models that he encountered

Mr Hofbauer. He was the Art Editor of Ivor and Nicholson 'but occasionally disguised himself as an evening student'. He came into the room where Quentin was posing and told him that the man in the adjoining room wanted to meet him. Quentin went next door and met the man in question. Though Quentin could not remember his name he had had quite an effect on him. When the class was over Mr Hofbauer suggested they visit one or two of the cafés he usually frequented in Charlotte Street. From this point on Quentin's whole social life changed. Up until then he said his evenings had been spent 'lying down recovering from the standing up' he had been doing all day, or writing, or darning his socks, or 'having a good cry'. Suddenly, he said, all these activities were squeezed out and he found himself spending two or three nights a week sitting in the cafés of Charlotte Street. This occupation represented far more than a change of pastime, it marked the discovery of a new self. To accompany his public face he began to construct a public character. He said he moved from 'concentrating on individuals to dealing with crowds'. In his youth his object had been 'to reform', now he said he wanted 'to entertain'. He was moving among people for whom his homosexuality was of no consequence at all. He began what he described as 'a whirlwind courtship of an entire district'. In appearance the cafés were just like those he had been barred from 15 years earlier in Old Compton Street, however the mood was very different. Though many homosexuals frequented them there was none of the high camp of Soho. Instead, he said, 'Despite the variety of classes, sexes, nationalities and callings there existed a kinship and spirit of genuine community.' It was this mix that Crisp looked back on with such fondness and it was the loss of this world that would later play a part in driving him across the Atlantic to New York, where he found a similar melting pot of peoples in New York's East Village where, he always maintained, everyone was his friend.

Quentin still dabbled in commercial art, designing the odd book jacket. He said he 'learned to handle books so they always fell open at the murder' and he soon perfected the art of reading through them rather than actually reading them. He was able to read a few sentences and from the way they were constructed judge the intended audience of the book and create the jacket accordingly. If his eye was caught by the words – 'her eyes filled with tears and her bosom rose and fell' – he said it was 'obvious the book was meant for women and the jacket was pastel shades with a dark-haired heroine with shallow cleavage'. If the novel had been written for men it would have said 'her huge breasts shuddered with emotion in their straitjacket of pink satin', and it would receive a cover in dark tones with a red-haired heroine with 'a deep cleavage'. If, in 300 pages, there was no mention of breasts at all, he assumed the volume must be documentary with 'no illustration' or for children with 'bright colours, [and a] mouse-haired heroine with no cleavage'. Among the firms for whom he worked most often was Ivor and Nicholson whose Art Editor told him that if he wanted to actually write something himself, now was the time. Quentin said that 'during the War there was a paper shortage so publishers would not print any old muck'. He decided to write a pamphlet in verse, mainly because he could not face doing anything too long. The idea had come to him some time before when a friend had uttered a limerick – about a kangaroo who offered himself to the zoo. It ended:

> *But whenever he tried,*
> *The committee replied,*
> *'We already have plenty of you.'*

By the time Quentin next saw his friend he had added a second verse:

> *'If you like you may leave us your name*
> *So that we may go into your claim*
> *And then doubtless you'll hear,*
> *In the course of the year,*
> *An evasive reply to the same.'*

Quentin said his friend now said that the limerick had become 'a slashing indictment of the Ministry of Labour'. Lacking any real experience, Quentin agreed and he developed it into what he would later call '48 rather clumsy verses of anger-less satire'. Not surprisingly, when he had finished it he quickly realised he needed something more to ensnare the publisher's interest. He said he 'set about trying to persuade Mr Peake to illustrate it'. Mr Peake was at that time the most fashionable illustrator in England. In spite of this he was a regular at the Bar-B-Q in Chelsea and was not in the least bit inaccessible. Quentin approached him, telling him that Ivor and Nicholson had already commissioned the book. Mr Peake declared himself, 'Willing to illustrate anything that was certain of appearing in print.' Thus Quentin was able to scurry back to the publishers and tell them he had secured his services. Quentin would later say that it was 'not the writing but his chicanery that secured the book's publication'. It was called *All This And Bevin Too* and was not a commercial success. Despite this he was commissioned to write another book. Unfortunately this one failed to even make it into print and Quentin sank back into oblivion.

Never get into a narrow double bed...

Never get into a narrow double bed with a wide single man.

Into this oblivion stepped a character who Quentin christened 'Barn Door' because, he said, he was as wide as one and 'as easily pushed to and fro'. Quentin met him late one night in one of his favourite cafés. 'The man looked undernourished and exhausted and was clearly homeless', and Quentin offered him a bed for the night. The next morning Quentin told him he could leave his possessions in the hall whilst he went looking for accommodation of his own. 'Three long, dark years later they were still there.'

At first, he said, their association consisted of meetings at Toni's or The Scala and afterwards, 'if he looked in need of sleep', Quentin would bring him home. After a while this progressed and, Quentin said, 'he formed the habit of visiting me every weekend and my life became a series of Saturdays for which I prepared and Sundays from which I recovered'. Adding wryly.

> *But I never gave up hope. I never let more than a few hours pass without including in the conversation the words 'When you have a room of your own ...' and I never gave him a latch key. I knew that once I had done that I was a lifer. I was entering the dank, dark prison of eternal love.*

Quentin said that because he

> *... could tell he had never known a world in which he had the upper hand, I became his slave. When presumably to normalise our relationship, he suggested a little sex, I concurred. A year or so later, in the middle of a sketchy embrace, he said, 'let's pack this in'; and I said 'let's'.*

Having lain alone for some 30 years Quentin said he found that he could not fully relax if he shared his bed with anybody, 'let alone someone of Barn Door's dimensions'. After a while Quentin and Barn Door found a solution to this problem and they took it in turns to sleep amongst the dust on the floor and to wake up in the morning more or less 'flock finished'. Quentin said,

> *The routine of my life was altered in areas which I thought were fixed for all time. I was obliged to shop and then I was obliged to cook. This I could only do by racial memory. I had never before gone further than to make toast when the bread had become too green to eat raw. Now I found myself clawing away at the carcasses of dead animals until my nails were full of blood and I felt like a mangy old sheep. I found that I had become so spinsterish that I was made neurotic not only by my life of domesticity but by the slightest derangement of my room. I would burst into a fit of weeping if the kettle was not facing due East.*

Quentin would say to me, when recalling the story of Barn Door, that the problem was that,

> *If you are going to have a relationship between two people one of you will inevitably adopt the part of the stooge, one of you will be left expressing amazement and amusement at jokes you have heard a thousand times. If you share a territory you will in the end only be left with the things about which you disagree. If you get up at six o'clock and your little friend gets up at six in the morning within a week you will take this for granted and you will say 'isn't it amazing, we agree'. But if your friend wants the soap on the left-hand side of the wash basin and you want it on the right. Divorce! And people will say you got divorced over a cake of soap? But they forget that you moved it EVERY DAY!'*

Resident Alien – The Play

Quentin said Barn Door's greatest problem was 'figuring out a way to pass the time' and that during their relationship he understood, for the first time, the purpose of the radio which Barn Door 'bathed himself' in every waking hour. 'It's function is not to entertain but to drown out the ticking of all clocks.' Quentin said,

Having myself spent so many happy hours alone, frequently doing nothing
but breathing I was bewildered to discover that for my friend spare time was an
imposition. If one event like Sunday lunch ended before another such as the movies
could begin he became distraught. He cleaned his shoes – yea, though they were
already like crimson glass, he put a new flint in his lighter, and he twiddled the
whistling, creaking, crackling knobs of our crotchety wireless set but, though he spent
his days picking and shovelling, the one thing he never did was to sit and dream.
In this respect I would have been tempted to say that he was ill did I not know
that health consists of having the same diseases as one's neighbours.

Anyway, 'shortly before one Easter holiday', Quentin told Barn Door that it
was time he visited his mother for at least a weekend. Quentin said,

These words touched Barn Door's sensibilities. He was deeply devoted to his
mother. He gathered up his things and left. And as he did so he said 'I don't see
what I've done wrong even now.'

Quentin said it was 'the saddest day of my life', before adding,

But then he married and had two children so he's one of my successes. …
I knew he was a Kinsey queer rather than a coot queer. He merely associated with
homosexuals because they bought their love by the pound. His idea of a courtship
was to take a few neolithic lurches towards the object of his desire. … He'd only
got his bulk to offer, he didn't understand a word that was said to him. But in
knowing him I came to know the whole world – there is no dark stranger.

The story of Barn Door would eventually become one of Quentin's most
famous anecdotes and one he was still recounting right up until the end of his
life. However cruel he may sound towards the man, I suspect it was not the
man who was his real target. Quentin's rage was against himself and the very
idea of cohabitation or 'nesting' as he called it. Equally he was recognising
that, for him, sex was never going to be successful. Perhaps this was because of
the fact that he wasn't really homosexual. Just six months before he died he
said this to me:

The life of a homosexual is so horrible that when I was young I couldn't believe it. It's not the social persecution it's what you are expected to do. I swanned around the West End looking wonderful and I thought 'Oh! I'm marvellous!' I didn't think what I had to do at the end of it. And when I learned I was so horrified I would have gone into a monastery. Does anyone want to take someone's penis into his mouth? It's so disgusting I couldn't bare it. Ohhh! Marlene Dietrich said you have to let them put it in otherwise they won't come back. Isn't that wonderful? She wanted praise not sex. Sex smudges your make-up. You see it's been explained to me at the age of 90 that I am not really a homosexual, I am a trans something or other, I can't remember what. I'm a woman in a man's body. If they'd had the operation to have it chopped off when I was younger I should have become a woman and I should have opened a knitting shop in Carlisle and no-one need ever have known my guilty secret and I should have been happy because I should have been part of life.

As ever, with Quentin, when he makes what may be a statement in deadly earnest there is a rather ludicrous rider – in this case the idea of Quentin Crisp ever living in Carlisle. However, I have no reason to disbelieve him when he talked of being a transsexual and many others recall him saying much the same thing. It also makes sense when one considers his constant complaint that it's impossible to find a 'real' gay man. What he means by this is perhaps a straight man, something he would have found as a 'woman'. Whatever, in his rejection of Barn Door, the only relationship of significance he ever spoke of in his mythologised life, he was waking up to the fact that 'as a tender comrade, faithful friend' he was a 'dead loss'. There would be no more 'nesting'.

If there is a heaven for homosexuals...

By heterosexuals the life after death is imagined as a world of light, where there is no parting. If there is a heaven for homosexuals, which doesn't seem very likely, it will be very poorly lit and full of people they can feel pretty confident they'll never have to meet again.

Quentin may have seen off Barn Door but Mr Hitler was proving more elusive and the War was going on and on. He maintained he was unworried by it saying, 'Perhaps because the First World War had left me so unmoved I didn't take the Second one very seriously.' More to the point:

Though some of the buildings in the city had been ruined, the people had been improved. Everyone talked to everyone – even to me. The golden age had temporarily arrived.

Not only had wartime prompted a greater openness in the British spirit it had had a marked effect on the women of London who, Quentin said, had 'gone butch'. They were driving trucks and doing all the jobs previously done by their men folk and to do this they had taken to wearing jackets, trousers and sensible shoes. This delighted Quentin as it meant he could now buy the footwear he had always liked best: black lace-up shoes with 'firm medium heels'. He said he became indistinguishable from a woman. Once, whilst waiting for a bus, a member of the constabulary, after looking him up and down, accused him of just that. Quentin reported the conversation as going something like this:

Policeman:	*What are you doing?*
Quentin:	*I'm waiting for a bus.*
Policeman:	*You're dressed as a woman.*
Quentin:	*I'm wearing trousers.*

Policeman:	*Woman wear trousers.*
Quentin:	*Are you blaming me because everyone else is so eccentric?*
Policeman:	*You're dressed as a woman and you'd better catch a bus quick or there will be trouble. People don't like that sort of thing.*

The policeman was correct. And, Quentin said, they could 'now add patriotism to other less easily named reasons' for hating him. On one occasion he was at Holborn station and, as he came up the escalator, he was followed by a group of men who proceeded to hit him with a blunt object until his face was covered in blood. Another time, he was set upon by a group of youths on a bus intent on 'deciding by fair means or foul' whether he was actually a man or a woman.

However the flip side to blackout life in London was that, by night, it was 'like one of those dimly lit parties that their hosts hope are slightly wicked'. Quentin said that, as soon as the bombs started to fall, the city 'became like a paved double bed' with voices whispering to you from dimly lit doorways. On one occasion he was returning by bus from an evening class in Willesdon and was joined at Notting Hill by an Australian soldier who sat down behind him. Without prompting the man took a comb from his pocket and proceeded to comb Quentin's hair all the way to Hyde Park Corner.

Alongside chance encounters there were the 'playgrounds' where boys met. One of these was on the towpath at Putney (still a much used cruising ground). The problem with these places was that, at first, they 'were known to only a few, then to the many, and then to the police'. At Putney they adopted the tactic of driving motor launches along the riverbank and shining torches into the undergrowth at which point 'men in all positions would hurl themselves at the floor'. Quentin was not a fan of these places, not because of some moral revulsion but because he 'did not want any liaison in conditions which might tend to obliterate my individuality'. He often quoted a Canadian actress: 'If the fuss is not about ourselves, then what the hell?'

On one of these twilight evenings he was sweeping along Ebury Street when he was stopped by a tall bearded gentleman who asked if he could photograph

Quentin. His name was Angus Macbean. A week later he went to his studios and the photographs were taken. Quentin said that he felt he was destined to meet Macbean, as he 'longed to take photographs as fervently as I wished to be photographed'. The most famous of these photos would feature on the title page of the brochure at Quentin's New York memorial. It's a stunning portrait, taken in 1941, of the young Quentin looking as a matinée idol. He is dressed smartly in shirt and tie, his eyelashes are long, and his features look delicately beautiful in the soft light. Though he stares straight at the camera, his eyes are trained downwards. The image captures Quentin's haughtiness and, crucially, his removedness. The subject is both absent and present: pleased to be photographed but remaining slightly aloof from the whole process. Similarly another of Macbean's pictures, this time shot in profile, gives the impression of a character not quite of this world.

Meantime life continued in the cafés of Fitzrovia, and Quentin was learning to polish his conversation skills further. It was this area of London that would become the kingdom described by Roland Camberton in the novel *Scamp* and, later still, by Maclaren-Ross in his memoirs. Quentin said that, 'as though we had the foreknowledge that we were living literature, we all set to work to become cameos'. They also set to work to 'live with style'. Many years later he would recount to me the story of one of the inhabitants of Fitzrovia who he thought had the most style:

> *She was a woman known as The Countess and, in spite of this, she had in fact no fixed address and no means of support and her body was perpetually bent double from a lifelong habit of looking in dustbins to see if she could find some-thing she could send to a kind friend or, if not, something she herself could use and, one day, in an expensive part of London she found a complete backless bead dress. She longed for dusk to fall so that she could nip into a dark doorway and try it on. Round about half past six her patience had worn out so she went into a churchyard in the middle of London and there she proceeded to take off her clothes. This caused a crowd to collect, and the crowd caused a policeman to collect, and the next day in court when the magistrate said 'and what exactly were you doing stripping amongst the dead?' She replied, 'I was doing what any women would be doing at that hour – changing for dinner.'*

Quentin always used her as proof that, in order to be stylish, you didn't need any actual money and the anecdote became part of his one-man show.

However, you did need money for bail, and it was bail Quentin would need when, for the first time, he was arrested for being himself.

What crime has in common with sport

What crime has in common with sport is that it fulfils every man's fantasy of plunging into the midst of terrible danger and surviving.

The incident occurred when Quentin was pursuing one of his favourite pastimes, buying shoes. He said he 'had systematically searched all the windows of Oxford Street and was just starting on Charing Cross Road' when he was stopped by two policemen and asked for his exemption papers. As always he showed them the one which said he was exempt on the grounds of 'sexual perversion'. The policemen weren't best pleased but allowed him to go on his way. However a couple of minutes later he bumped into an old friend and 'part-time hooligan' by the name of Mr Palmer. Quentin 'slapped on his plate his ration of eternal wisdom for the day' and turned into Coventry Street when the policemen reappeared. 'Just a moment you, we are taking you in for soliciting.'

'This was an eventuality that I and my enemies had expected ever since the far-off days when I had first been questioned by police.' He was marched off to Saville Row police station and was searched by one man whilst others stood around saying 'mind how you go'. His pockets were emptied and he was 'sufficiently unzipped to establish that he wasn't wearing women's undergarments'. He was then asked to find someone who could provide bail. He proceeded to give the police a list of names, but they insisted on having only one, so he gave the name of his ballet teacher friend but, unfortunately, she wasn't in. Not until ten o'clock that night was he allowed to call someone else – the gentleman who had been responsible for the kangaroo limerick – who promptly arrived and set him free.

Quentin hurried out into the blacked out streets of London to track down Mr Palmer to ask him to appear at Bow Street magistrate's court the next morning to testify that he knew Quentin. He then went to Toni's to round up his friends as character witnesses. Many told him to have the case postponed and engage the services of a solicitor but he refused saying that, if he did and was found guilty, the sentence he would receive would be much harsher. 'Justice revenges herself not only on those who commit crimes but on those who take up her time.' Having secured his character witnesses he collapsed into bed exhausted.

The next morning he said he 'dressed in black and marched to Bow Street'. He said that as soon as he stepped into the courtroom he was assailed by two contrary feelings. The first was

> ... *that here was the long-awaited fully-involving situation to which I could summon all my capacity for survival, and the second was that I might fall on the floor in a dead faint and that it might be just as well if I did.*

Despite the fact that he had appeared in court many times as a character witness for others in the same situation, this time he was there on trial and it was completely different. Quentin had totally forgotten that the Magistrate would just sit behind the bench expressionless whilst his Clerk conducted the whole case. Quentin was amazed at how benign the Magistrate was and by how 'bitchy' the Clerk was 'turning slowly towards the public, with his hands in the air like George Sanders uttering his best lines'. At one point, turning to the gallery for approval, he had asked, 'You are a male person I presume?' Not since the sarcasm of the doctors at his army medical had Quentin been subjected to such humiliation. The police acted in what was a largely standard way for this type of case saying that, between the hours of this and that, they saw Quentin speak to various people who they said had 'all looked horrified'. When the police had completed their evidence, Quentin was asked if he would prefer to reply from the dock or from the witness box, where he would have to take the oath. He chose the latter not, he said, because he thought invoking the spirit of 'you-know-who' might help his case, but because the witness box was raised above the courtroom and 'gave him a better stage from which to perform his defence'. It also, he said, meant he did not have to have his back to the audience for his big scene which he had decided to play dead straight 'like Imogen in *Cymbeline*'.

When his defence began he adopted a surprising, though extremely canny, tone that he would use in many contexts throughout his life. Far from pointing out that the two policemen were complete liars, he humbly pointed out that he thought they had been mistaken in their assumptions and in their interpretation of the events they had seen, and that their error had been prompted by having read his exemption paper which described him as a homosexual. (In later life he would adopt a similar tactic when someone asked him to go or do something he did not want to. Rather than say 'no' outright, he would say 'I am not worthy'. That way, he said, they didn't dislike him for rejecting them and it wasn't until much later they realised that was exactly what he had done.) To this end, Quentin went on to say to the Magistrate that he felt the policeman had misinterpreted his appearance. He said he dressed and looked as he did in order that the whole world could see he was homosexual so that it would 'set him apart from the rest of the human race rather than enabling him to form a contract of any kind with it'. 'Who,' he asked the magistrate, 'could hope to solicit anybody in broad daylight in a crowded London street looking as I do?' (He was later told by one one of his friends that, at this point, a stranger in the public gallery was heard to say, 'They can't do nothing with it. He can't 'elp 'isself. You can see that.') Following Quentin's performance various people went into the box to testify to his character. Each one was asked by the Magistrate's Clerk if they knew he was a homosexual and each replied that they did. The question was each time followed by the words, 'And yet you describe him as respectable?' All said, 'Yes.'

By this stage Quentin said that the Magistrate was 'tired of this recital of praise and promptly dismissed the case on account of insufficient evidence'. Quentin was free and he had been freed not because of legal wrangling but because he had told the truth; it was a remarkable day indeed. It further solidified in his mind the concept that, whatever the world threw at him, he must above all remain true to himself.

Quentin may have defeated His Majesty's constabulary in court but outside the courtroom things were very different and they soon took their revenge. Systematically they began to make sure he was barred from every public house in Fitzrovia, eventually even from his regular haunt The Wheatsheaf. Quentin's friends protested but the landlord pointed out that it was a choice between having Quentin in the building or having a licence to serve anyone else. (The police had accused him of running a 'funny kind of place' and when he'd said 'how funny?' – had pointed at Quentin.) Quentin said he was forced to 'take the veil of abstinence' which didn't worry him; but he was also forced to forego half his audience, which did. Just when he thought things couldn't get worse, they did. Peace broke out.

The stately homos of England

I am now one of the stately homos of England.

Quentin described the night that the end of the War was declared as a 'terrible evening'. 'Death made-easy' vanished overnight and soon love 'made easy' (personified by the American GI soldiers) also disappeared. But more than anything Quentin regretted the fact that 'even mere friendship grew scarce'. Quentin said that 'Londoners now started to regret the indiscriminate expansiveness' they had shown during the War and returned 'to their old ways'. He also said that he felt that people's attitude to him changed. During the War he had been 'a landmark more cheerful looking and more bomb proof than St Paul's Cathedral' but now he felt he was merely a reminder of the 'unfairness of fate: he was still alive whilst the brave and the beautiful had gone'. All these unwelcome interruptions combined with another problem, for the first time Quentin felt he was getting old. He said his friends were delighted 'and did not resist the temptation to nudge him towards the grave with the odd straight talk'. One of his friends said, 'You are dying your hair in order to seem younger!' This was not true as Quentin had used henna since he was 24, but 'as my life was one long journey towards self-assessment I felt I must always give consideration to the opinions of me held by other people, however malicious'.

He set about forcing the red out and the 'blue' in. This would allow him to continue his original purpose of showing the world that he dyed his hair 'deliberately' but also that underneath the tinting he was grey haired and so he was not doing it in order to look younger. During this transition phase, which lasted for about six months, Quentin said he passed from 'doubtful youth to unmistakable middle age' and became 'one of the stately homos of England'. He was entering what he termed his 'blue period'. He said that when he entered this phase in his life people's attitude to him changed, not because they had seen the light but because he was perceived to no longer constitute a threat. Without my scarlet hair 'I was like a Westerner without a gun', he said.

Shortly after entering his 'blue period' he developed eczema, and his face broke out in a terrible rash. Friends said it was an allergy of some kind – 'If it was an allergy,' Quentin said. 'It was to middle age.' – and it was something from which he suffered throughout his life and which would cause him a huge amount of pain in later years.

> *Because of eczema large parts of my body have to be swathed in these wretched bandages to prevent me from clawing myself until the blood gushes out of my wounds and down the stairs with a gurgling sound. Mr Eliot wrote that it is 'love that weaves the intolerable shirt of flame' but I'm wearing it and I think its eczema.*

Resident Alien – The Play

During the next few years he lost his appetite for art school modelling. 'There seemed to be no new schools within reach to go to and no new positions to try that could be held for long enough for the students to draw them.' Later, he would add, 'I became aware that being a model was a profession at which after the first year or two I could not get better. I was bound to get worse.' Quentin felt he was growing old.

> *It was as though I had been climbing a hill in expectation of finding on the other side a landscape utterly different from the one which I had passed. Now I was at the summit I could see what stretched ahead was exactly the same as what lay behind.*

Quentin would later say,

> *For an introvert his environment is himself and can never be subject to startling or unforeseen change. My failures to win true love, to stay in the movie industry, to write books that anyone would publish were not a series of unconnected accidents to*

which I was prone because of my exposed position in society. They were the expression of my character – the built-in concomitant of a morbid nature to which dreams were more vivid than reality. The infinitesimally small success that I had known had been achieved inevitably in terms of being rather than doing. I had gained what I had aimed for when I first got control of my own life. But in middle age physical well-being faded. Money, fame, wisdom are the booby prizes of the elderly, I had never been able to win. My preoccupation with happiness had been total. I would not yet describe myself as miserable but I was deflated.

Quentin was going through a sort of a mid-life crisis (though I'm sure it's a term he would have hated) and, for the first time, openly contemplating mortality. 'I can never get it into my head that I shall one day die,' he had once said to a friend. He had replied, 'Neither can I, but I practise like mad.'

Quentin was unmistakably middle-aged. 'In the gay world by the time you can no longer be referred to as a boy you've had it. I knew someone of 43 who still held out to being a boy.'

Bored of modelling he took a job in an art department of a publishing house. He said the place was like a 'cross between an Antonioni film and a St James's Street club'. However, everyone was treated kindly, even by their superiors, and no-one was ever sacked. Quentin said,

Finding it impossible to take any further interest in myself because I had exhausted all the potentialities of my character, I decided, since I was suddenly surrounded by new people in a new setting that I would devote some of my attention to them. It wasn't easy.

His Art Editor had noticed this trait in him and asked, 'What do you hold with, apart from yourself?' Quentin said he racked his brains but couldn't think of a thing. His old friend, the New York performance artist Penny Arcade, would later tell me of conversations she had had with people who knew Quentin at this time and who described him as 'self-obsessed and at times downright mean'.

Quentin stayed at the publishing house for two and a half years, invoking a policy that remained with him throughout his life, that is, spending only half of what he earned. He said it meant he would only have to work for half his time on earth. As a result when he came to leave the publishing house he felt rich enough not to work for a whole year and he decided to write a novel.

Three reasons for becoming a writer

There are three reasons for becoming a writer. The first is that you need the money; the second, that you have something to say that you think the world should know; and the third is that you can't think what to do with the long winter evenings.

Quentin said, 'I had only the latter and I suspect that's why the publisher didn't like the book. It was promptly rejected.' As Quentin himself observed he was

… not really suited to writing a novel, as Mr Forster said novelists presuppose a world of people interested in human relationships. My trouble was not merely that I was uninterested in them. I didn't think they existed. I tried to write without the literary convention of love and in the words of one publisher's reader, to succeed in doing this would require genius or at least style.

Another comment he received is that they were 'satire without anger'. Quentin would later say:

I now know if you describe things as better than they are you are considered to be romantic: if you describe things as worse than they are, you will be called a realist: and if you describe them exactly as they are you will be thought of as a satirist and this was the only sense in which my book was a satire.

Quentin also noted: 'As there were no sympathetic characters in real life there were none in my book.' But, the most obvious reason for his lack of success was that he was a bad writer or, at the very least, a writer still in search of a voice. He continued to hawk the book around London until eventually he had exhausted all options and it sat in a brown parcel in his room, a reminder of his failure, to be moved around every time he wanted to sit down. Whether the brown parcel element of the story is true or not, yet again he succeeds in dramatising and mythologising an element of his life. One could well imagine a character from a Samuel Beckett play who was forced to move round a physical reminder of his failure every single day. The net result was that Quentin was compelled to return to the world of conventional work.

He managed to get a job with a firm making display cases for exhibitions and the next four years were spent doing bits and pieces, none of which took him any nearer to his dream of being recognised. However, in the outer world things were changing and the mists of repression were slowly lifting. The ban on Quentin in the old pubs was lifted and his acceptibilty increased to such a level that on one occasion a gentleman was asked to leave The Coach and Horses for making fun of him. Quentin said that when this happened he knew for sure that 'Soho had become a reservation for hooligans'. It was during one of his regular visits to 'The Coach' that he encountered a young woman who said, 'Why don't you come and talk to our lot?' Quentin said he would 'talk to anyone who could not get away' but that he 'wouldn't talk for long about anything other than myself'. Quentin was dispatched to speak to a group of doctors.

He quickly found that giving a talk had its own technique and, as often in his life, when he returned from the experience he sat down and processed it, trying to work out how to do it better next time. The doctors, however, were sufficiently pleased with his address to ask him questions afterwards. One told Quentin that he was about to embark on a survey of homosexuals. Quentin said that 20 years earlier he would have thought this 'a noble survey' but now he 'had to fight hard not to sigh'. But he didn't; and he answered the doctor's questions as best he could. However, on his way out one man couldn't resist making a dig at Quentin, saying 'I think it's a pity you dress the way you do though ...'. Quentin said that, once again, he felt he was reading that paragraph which seemed to occur regularly in books about sexual abnormality which began: 'There is no need to waste time considering that small group of men who dress and act in an effeminate manner ....' Things were changing for homosexuals, but for men who wished to exist in the ungoverned territory between male and female, effeminate homosexuals, much continued to remain unchanged.

After his visit to the doctors, Quentin was in a café one night when a friend of his inquired as to why it had been arranged. Quentin said that, before he was able to reply, another friend had interrupted, 'Well Quentin has a problem of adjusting himself to society and he ....' The sentence was never finished for his other friend interjected, 'I don't agree. Quentin does exactly as he pleases. The rest of us have to adapt ourselves to him.' Despite the fact that the interchange was based on a predictable misunderstanding Quentin later said this remark seemed to 'outline a great dilemma'. He said that

> ... almost all the psychological ills a man can suffer spring from self-doubt. Once this is removed, his troubles vanish, but if anyone really came to believe that he was wise, witty, kind and beautiful, think what troubles his friends would have.

Wth his career as a novelist in ruins Quentin now embarked on a brief spell as a writer of musical theatre. A guitarist friend had asked him to write the book for a musical. Quentin inquired what type of story the man was looking for; he replied 'a simple boy meets girl' type. Quentin said he didn't know any boys who met girls and suggested instead a horror story – to be called *Carry On Hearse!* or *The Thing And I*. He had great fun writing this and liked working collaboratively, as opposed to the isolation of his previous artistic incarnation as a novelist. Unfortunately, despite an enjoyable process, the man didn't understand Quentin's jokes and Quentin 'didn't understand the music'. 'It all seemed to me the maximum amount of noise conveying the minimum amount of information.' Nevertheless Quentin thought of this as a 'happy disaster'. Instead of labouring away alone he was able to show off before his collaborator. 'Indeed a large part of our time was spent jumping up and down and proclaiming each other's greatness.' Also, he said, failure was no longer depressing him because he was becoming used to it.

> Each unsuccessful attempt at fame was bringing me closer to the time when triumph would be useless even if it came. I had gradually become more or less immune to feeling of every kind and to disappointment in particular. I had been hit in the same place too often.

He had also learned the trick of dealing with unsuccessful events: tell everyone about them and turn them into amusing anecdotes. Words were becoming a way of healing the wounds inflicted on him by experience.

He went back to modelling, and he was to learn that in this arena too things were changing. Though only four years had gone by since he had last been a full-time model the landscape had altered beyond his belief. During the War things had been a little haphazard but now, Quentin said, 'The students enrolled for chaos. The young people wandered through the corridors in droves, shouting, cursing, singing and necking.' Whilst the amount of opportunity for life drawing had increased their interest in it had dwindled. 'In the galleries to which they visited they saw almost no paintings of naked girls flopping on cushions.' The future, as they saw it, did not lie in painting Quentin and his sudden arrival in the room seemed to indicate a return to something outmoded and old-fashioned. If being treated with little respect was now the daily currency for most models, for Quentin this became open contempt and, despite the massive social changes taking place in the world outside, paradoxically those with least reason to be shocked by Quentin's appearance were now turning on him. In some schools this led to open shouts about his private life and to students hanging out of the windows to mock his appearance as he arrived. And in the world outside he was again finding himself criticised, not because his appearance represented sin – for he felt that the notions of good and evil, innocence and sin were becoming blurred – but because, he said,

It was no longer my wickedness that annoyed them, it was my pomposity – my insistence on taking the blame for something on which judgment was no longer passed.

Coincidently, the symbols he had adopted 40 or so years earlier in order to clearly express and delineate his sexual type had now become, in part, the uniform of many young people. Quentin said that by growing his hair long and wearing outlandishly bright colours he had merely become the 'oldest teenager in town'.

I inadvertently gave the impression of trying to gate crash a Kings Road party for

people two generations younger than myself. I was not merely a stopped clock, I was a stopped grandfather clock.

There was nothing he could do about it, though.

It was much too late for me to return to the human race I had left in childhood. I would have had no idea how to go on in the presence of real people as their equal. If I had originally been a member of their club, I had certainly never paid my dues and as Macbeth would have said 'I was in tinsel stepped in so far that, should I wade no more, returning were as tedious as go-er'.

Quentin sought salvation in the cinema. Here in the darkened rooms and the magical lighted world of the movies, the 'forgetting chamber' as he would later refer to it, he was transported to another world. He started to live what he called a 'rich life by proxy'. However, his essential puritanism kicked in and going to the cinema seemed, in a way, indecent. Quentin said that in order to minimise his guilt at going to the pictures alone – his fear was that God would plunge his arm through the roof of the cinema if he went there on his own – he would take a friend and then at least he could say when asked what he was doing there that he was 'accompanying my friend'. Quentin would manage to go to the cinema at least once a week for many years, sometimes he would even go on consecutive days or see two films in one day thus spending 'seven hours out of 24 in the forgetting chamber'. He said that real life became for him

… like a series of those jarring moments when the screen goes blinding white, the jagged edge of a torn strip of film flicks one's eye-balls and there is a flash of incomprehensible numerals lying on their sides (like a message in code from Hades) before the dream begins again.

He never refused to see any film, unless it was an English one. He was mainly a devotee of 'the divine woman'. 'In my lifetime she changed three times, first she called herself Brigitte Helm later Greta Garbo and finally Marlene Dietrich.' Quentin said he thought about her a great deal 'wore her clothes, said her sphinx-like lines and ruled her kingdom'. He came to the conclusion that beauty was not a girl but an 'Aryan face seen through Semitic eyes' and that this was what gave her the tragic and remote quality that became her hallmark.

Quentin said that these were the last generation of movie stars and that the fault lies '... not in our stars. But in ourselves ...'. The beauties of the last generation symbolised hopeless love. 'Now it is too late for tears. What modern man has time to play a guitar under his true love's window or the energy to climb up the ivy into her room?' Instead Quentin said someone had invented 'espresso sex and to serve this tasteless concoction there had to be a mechanical doll whose only recommendation was her infinite availability'. He felt the woman who came to embody this ideal most strongly was Marilyn Monroe whose directors 'pursued her to flaunt her astonishing sexual equipment before us with the touching defencelessness of a retarded child'. Quentin said she was what 'the modern man desires most in life, a mistress who could be won without being wooed. She was the football pool of love'. Yet again Quentin was proving himself the romantic nihilist.

Cinema going however remained a lifelong obsession, though his focus shifted as the cinema changed in nature and the delineation between good and evil became less clearly defined. He said that when movie ethics became too confusing for him he ceased to bother about them and turned his attention to the technique of film construction. However,

> *Before long, even this interest was snatched from me by the modern passion for the haphazard — for the abandonment of style. When Antonioni ascended the celluloid throne, pictures became as boring as being alive.*

After almost 20 years in the twilight zone he came blinking back into the light of day.

There ought to be a Ministry of Death

There ought be a Ministry of Death you know.

By the time 1963 had come along Quentin was 55 and, he said, quite ready for nuclear oblivion. The Cuban missile crisis was just around the corner and *Time* magazine had confidently predicted that 1963 would be the year when the 'missile gap' was at its widest and when the enemy would strike. Quentin asserted that it wasn't the nuclear oblivion that worried him but the uncertainty about when it would arise. He offered a solution:

There ought to be a Ministry of Death you know, though in Orwellian terminology, I suppose it would be named the Ministry of Heaven. It would be an august body of men all preferably under 30 years of age who would deal with the chore of exterminating old people. Before everything else they would have to agree upon a limit (say 60) to live beyond which would be an offence (punishable with life?) Then the Ministry would have to make sure that, six months before his 60th birthday, every living being received a notice of post-dated congratulations advising him which town hall he would be required to visit on the happy occasion. A week before his final birthday he would receive a final notice and then, at the glorious hour, unless he preferred to walk there on his own two feet, the van would call to take him to oblivion. In America this vehicle would be painted to look like a fiery chariot but in England it would be plain blue with the words 'Ministry of Death, Kensington Branch' discreetly lettered on the side. For the first few years there might be undignified scenes, but in Britain individual liberty is so often curtailed for the common good that order would soon prevail. If the government does not soon adopt some plan such as I have outlined, I shall have to put into action a more personal scheme for limiting my span of years. I shall commit a murder. This is something that for a long time I have wanted to do. It would be impossible to get through the kind of life I have known without accumulating a vast stockpile of rage. Whenever people read in the papers that someone has purchased a machine gun and mowed down a whole neighbourhood, they invariably say, 'I wonder what brought that on'. They even make some such remark when the subject is an American Negro. To me the motive is self-evident. Mass murderers are simply people who have had ENOUGH! Someone once asked me to what I attributed my longevity and I replied 'Bad luck'. It's true. I'm ready for death but I just won't die. I once sat opposite a little old lady in a train carriage near Bromley and overheard her say to someone '... and then after 25 years, my husband died'. I was just about to look gravely at the floor when she added 'and oh, the relief'. I understand her utterly.

Resident Alien – The Play

Whilst there is clearly a strong comic element to this concept it would be wrong to dismiss it as merely a trifle, as with much of what Quentin said there was an elaborate treble bluff going on and, I believe, he at least in part meant it. This technique was central to Quentin's mode of speaking, what came to be known as 'Crisperanto'. When he spoke his audience had to be constantly on their guard because, despite his assertion that he only ever said what he meant, as much of the meaning was conveyed in tone as it was in substance. For example in the eighties when he famously dismissed Aids as a 'fad' many people took this comment at face value and felt he had completely 'let the side down'. He may have done, but he may equally have been satirising the media themselves and their 'here today, gone tomorrow' attitudes to subjects in vogue. I say this because I felt that often what Quentin said depended upon the person he was speaking to, and the content and tone was influenced by what he believed their values to be. There were times during my interview with him when I felt he was deliberately saying things he felt I wouldn't agree with merely to provoke me. It was as if, whenever he felt you were getting close to him, he had to push you away. Perhaps the intimacy denied him in his youth, and which he never found with a partner, meant that it was one of the things he feared most. He wanted to be listened to but, it seemed to me, feared merely being liked. He needed an audience but would never himself join them in the stalls, instead remaining safely behind the footlights. To him, conversation was a kind of elaborate sword fight in which sentences had to be continually sharpened and subjects prodded and poked in order to reveal the truth. Even when he was speaking about what appeared to be his most deeply held beliefs there was a detached quality to his performance, a kind of stridency with a twinkle in the eye, the wicked fairy on the rock casting spells over his followers.

So whilst the 'wicked fairy' waited for nuclear oblivion he decided to take a different tack with regard to his career in the, now, unfashionable business of 'posing' and he turned his attentions to portrait classes. This was thought amongst models to be something of a come down but Quentin felt he had no choice – when he had recently visited the dentist with tooth decay he had been told that it wasn't his teeth that were decaying, it was his whole body. However he found that when he returned to portrait classes he was no longer at home.

I had never been legally married to real life. Between the ages of 22 and 40 I had merely conducted an illicit liaison with it. In taking up modelling once more it transpired that I had gone home to another culture once too often.

He made another desperate effort to get a full-time job but to no avail. Now it was not only his odd appearance which went against him but his age. All doors were shut. He retired to his filthy room and wrapped himself in his dirty dressing gown.

I fell back into the oubliette of art. In its Havisham twilight I was grimly at home. About me there was something of the dusty elaboration of her mouse-nibbled wedding cake. So here, propped up on some rickety Victorian chair, I sat silent and I hope, apparently resigned – an ashy clinker from the long dead fires of Bohemia.

He wondered what had happened, what went wrong. He saw his life as an 'unholy dash between cradle and grave'. No-one had ever been in love with him and he had never been in love with anyone. He didn't even know what the expression meant. He remembered a story he had read in a newspaper some years earlier. It involved two brothers who lived in a New York house and never went out. One of them was blind and partially paralysed which meant the other had to leave the house to buy food and newspapers. The room was piled high with books transforming the place into a network of canyons and, to keep intruders out, every inch of it was mined with booby traps. One day, one of these went off and when, many months later, the corpses of the brothers were found, one of them was still sitting up in bed waiting for the other. The second lay only a few yards away pinned by tons of newsprint to the floor. The rats had begun to gnaw at his body. In a sense Quentin felt this was the way he lived: this the fate that had overtaken him. 'The place where no harm can come is the place where nothing at all can come' and this was where he stood or, more precisely, sat.

He said power was what he craved most. He wanted 'dominance over others in order to redress the balance'. A lifetime of being constantly at the mercy of others had left him crushed 'and seething with a lust for tyranny'. He said he was stumbling towards his grave 'confused, hurt and hungry'. But then an event occurred which no-one could have foreseen and which was to be the first stage on the journey to the life he longed for and which no-one, not even he, could have dreamed at the age of 58 would ever come to him.

I have entered the profession of being

I have entered the profession of being.

One afternoon, whilst wrapped in his filthy dressing gown and staring at his grubby gas fire, Quentin received a visitor. It was Philip O'Connor. Quentin hadn't seen him for the best part of 15 years when he too had been a 'full-time hooligan member' of the Fitzrovia bohemian set. In those days Quentin said Mr O'Connor had spent his time touring the public houses and cafés of the area 'spouting improvised doggerel to friends and strangers alike without ever hoping or even wishing to be understood'. However, in the intervening years he had written *The Memoirs Of A Public Baby* and the instant fame this had brought him had introduced him to the BBC's Third Programme. It was at the behest of the BBC that he had come to see Quentin. The Third Programme was planning a piece on eccentrics and Mr O'Connor wanted Quentin to feature. Quentin wanted to know if there was money in it and when Mr O'Connor confirmed there was he immediately agreed to take part.

According to Quentin there and then Mr O'Connor went out into the street to his motor car and returned with a huge box of recording equipment. Quentin recalled him then holding a microphone up in front of his face and asking him to 'say something about life and death'. Quentin said, '[I] spoke and spoke and only when the machine ran out of tape did I stop.' Quentin said that Mr O'Connor then left, seemingly pleased with the result. Quentin however set little store by this. He was used to the bohemian life of the Charlotte Street set, a life in which people were always 'just about to be on the stage or in a film or write a book'.

I couldn't really believe that anyone, let alone myself who had forged such a strong link with dreamy Bohemia could ever establish a working relationship with the real world, let alone the BBC.

He was wrong – it was to be the turning point of his professional life.

Not only did the programme get the go ahead but, a few days later, Mr O'Connor returned to Quentin's room with his boss to do more recordings. Quentin claimed to have never listened to the programme when it was finally broadcast, but then many years later he also claimed not to have read my play when I sent it to him. 'I've received it but I haven't read it,' he declared. However Phillip Ward, the Executor of his will, later told me he had read it. Perhaps this was another element of the inbuilt Crisp self-defence mechanism, a feigned indifference to anything that may wound him in any way. Whether Quentin did or didn't listen to the programme, it was a success; and shortly following its broadcast he received an offer he could not refuse.

He was told that a publisher who had heard the show had said he 'ought to write a book'. Quentin said that people were always making such comments 'even if you only told one funny joke a year', but 'if the person was a publisher you should take it seriously'. This time, Quentin said, the man in question was William Kimber who 'published any number of books by disused colonels and the memoirs of a lot of extinct district nurses'. Quentin nervously called him and Kimber hesitantly admitted that 'the words had indeed fallen from his lips'. He told Quentin that if he wrote a 2,000-word synopsis of his autobiography he would read it and then decide if he could offer him a contract. Quentin agreed, and set to work immediately with renewed vigour. His writing career, which he thought was over before it ever began, was suddenly given a second chance.

Unfortunately, as Quentin said, 'even a little of my life seemed too much for Mr Kimber'. He wrote Quentin a courteous letter saying that if he published a book based on the incidents Quentin had described he would be 'bombarded from all directions with libel suits'. Quentin said he could not understand this – though he was endlessly outspoken about his own failings, he was seldom indiscreet about the failings of others. However a lifetime of literary let-downs meant that Quentin was not surprised at the reaction and he returned to modelling, thinking that that really was it as far as writing was concerned.

That was until he went on a modelling assignment to the Home Counties which was, by now, one of the few places still willing to employ him. During the journey he struck up a conversation with a fellow passenger who he entertained with a few of his stories, in particular the story of Mr Kimber and the book that never was. 'It just so happened' said Quentin, that the gentleman was 'married to Thames and Hudson' and said he would contact some of his spies and attempt to 'do what Mr Kimber had failed to do'. Within a few days the man contacted Quentin and introduced him to his first Literary Agent who he described as 'a Catholic Texan married to a Protestant Irish woman living in Putney'. He was instantly taken with Quentin and he took the 2,000-word synopsis and quickly submitted it, along with two photographs of Quentin, to the publisher Jonathan Cape. Within days Quentin was given a contract and £100. He couldn't believe his luck.

Initially he wanted to call his book *I Reign In Hell*:

> *I believed that the readers, having perused the first few pages would be convinced I had indeed based much of my life on that of Mr Lucifer by refusing to serve in heaven (respectable society).*

However the title was rejected and from a number of possibilities *The Naked Civil Servant* was chosen. The name came to him following a conversation with a journalist from *The Scotsman* newspaper. During the interview the man asked Quentin if he was a famous model. Quentin explained that there was no longer such a thing as a 'famous model', as the painting of nude models was out of fashion. He told him that the relationship between artists and their models had ceased to be a cause of 'prurient speculation not because newspapers and their readers had changed their attitudes but because painters no longer worked from the nude', and the only people who did were in the schools and they were engaged by the term and their wages ultimately came from the Minister of Education. He told him they were just like Civil Servants except that 'during office hours they were naked'.

Quentin later said the title of the book was a terrible mistake as everywhere he went he was forced to explain it. Indeed right up to his death journalists were misinterpreting the title and claiming he had once been a Civil Servant in the traditional sense. However, the title did have one advantage which was brought home to him forcibly when a friend recounted a visit to her mother. The woman noticed, on entering her mother's chintzy living room, a copy of the book lying on the coffee table. Amazed she asked her mother, 'Whatever made you buy that?' Her mother, rather taken aback, replied, 'I don't know why you are looking so shocked, I've always been interested in the Civil Service.'

The book was published in 1968 and was a big success. For a while it even entered the bestseller list. After his previous three literary failures he had finally discovered his voice or, more accurately, married his speaking voice to his literary one. Also he had found a subject which chimed with the times. *The Naked Civil Servant* appealed to the Swinging Sixties' generation with its wit and above all else, Quentin thought, 'its scandal value'. Quentin said 'The sixties' youth, led to victory by the Beatles' had inherited the earth a few years before *The Naked Civil Servant* came out. For the first time the younger generation had wealth and with it came freedom, freedom to set fashions, not only in what to see, hear, and view, but in what to say. Sex, of course, was at the top of their shopping list and became the favourite subject for discussion, 'homo' sex was thought even more exciting given the fact that it had only been legalised 'between consenting adults and in private' the year before and the legislation was still passing through Parliament. Quentin said,

If to be a man of destiny is to arrive at a point in history when the only gift you have to offer has suddenly become relevant, then in this tiny and purely social way that is what for the moment I became.

But, more importantly, he was fully embracing the person he had become and putting his unique experiences down on paper. He had discovered that his most remarkable gift was himself and from here on in he could enter 'the profession of being'.

But when the book first hit the streets the reviews were decidedly mixed. Quentin said that 'at best they were kind, at worst contradictory'. One said it was 'full of self-pity', another commented on it's 'freedom from self-pity'; one was delighted with the aphorisms, *The Times Literary Supplement* disliked the 'arch and jaunty style'. Quentin said he didn't reject the criticism

> *… on the fatuous grounds that it is prompted by unworthy motives or that to care about it is in some way beneath me. I hold that the very purpose of existence is to reconcile the glowing opinions we hold of ourselves with the appalling things that other people think about us.*

Despite this self-deprecation *The Naked Civil Servant* did strike a strong note with the mood of the times. Its opening line sets the tone for what is an unflinching look at his life:

> *From the dawn of history I was so disfigured by the characteristics of a certain kind of homosexual person that, when I grew up, I realised that I could not ignore my predicament.*

Paul Robinson in his excellent essay, *The Stately Homo*, describes Quentin as the 'classic unreliable narrator whose passion to entertain is forever sabotaging his duty to inform'. And, to some extent, this is perhaps true. Quentin is given to comic exaggeration and there are clearly times in the book when his desire for comic effect runs roughshod over the actual reporting of the facts. But this in no way diminishes the brutal honesty of feeling that his words convey. Towards the end of the final chapter he says:

> *No-one has ever been in love with me even faintly – even for half an hour, or if they have, it was a well-kept secret. Yet I can write this sentence with nothing more than a feeling of wounded vanity. I experience no keen sense of loss because I, myself, was never in love with anyone and do not clearly know what the expression means.*

The book is a strange contradiction; pitiful, in the dictionary sense of the word, that is deserving pity but utterly without self-pity. Quentin tells you what he did, tells you what he feels, but never once directly blames anyone else. Indeed, he often shifts the blame onto himself, too much so for some critics who see this as an example of his internalised homophobia. Its outlook is at best stoical and at worst downright pessimistic, yet the defiantly sardonic tone of the writing makes the reading of it a curiously uplifting experience and an understandable beacon for outcasts everywhere.

The hardback edition of the book sold out its run of around 3,500 copies and Quentin received around £300. The financial success or failure of the book, however, was not the point. Quentin said the important thing was

> *... another chunk of the wall against which I had so long been leaning had given way ... through the aperture thus created I could now see a tantalising corner of the arena that I longed to enter.*

Almost a month after his autobiography was published he was interviewed on television for the first time.

The survival of the glibbest

Remember that on television only one law prevails: the survival of the glibbest.

The interview came about by a rather circuitous route. The 'inhabitants of the kingdom of Bohemia', as Quentin was fond of calling them, had thrown a party to celebrate the success of *The Naked Civil Servant*. It took place in a restaurant in Charlotte Street. The guests were people Quentin knew or, more often than not, only slightly knew. One such man was a 'minor televisionary' who on leaving promised Quentin he would 'see what he could do for me'. As a result Quentin found himself on the then famous, but now defunct, BBC show *Late Night Line Up*.

The show was a panel discussion. The other members of the panel were a monk and the television chef Fanny Craddock. Quentin said he immediately took to her. She was a seasoned pro when it came to self-promotion and appearing on television and the degree of animation she put into her performance impressed the debutant greatly. When the time came for his appearance he was waiting backstage with a researcher who asked him three times if he was nervous. Quentin replied, 'No, why would I be, what have I got to lose?' He would later admit that this was, in truth, a defensive answer, he was nervous and must have known that if he blew it he would not be asked back. As he went on he told himself that above all he must avoid opening his answers with the words 'well' or 'er'. He had also decided to try and survive whatever was said to him without displaying 'embarrassment or shock'.

He needn't have worried. The questions were fairly bland involving his appearance and his domestic arrangements. They were the same questions he would go on to answer for the rest of his life on such occasions and, indeed, he became so seasoned in the art that he took to writing and talking about television with great lucidity.

Looked at from the front the television screen appears to be a lighted rectangle full of celebrities and other disasters. Seen from behind, it is an arid waste in which, like farmers in a dust bowl, broadcasters and producers dig for something, anything on which to feed their bleating flocks. Television has so much spare time that everyone will be on it in the end. When you go on TV, as you will because Mr Warhol has promised everyone his 15 minutes, you should treat your appearance like a geography exam. The night before your exam you open your atlas at random and if it says China you learn everything there is to know about China and if the next day the main question in your paper is France, your answer begins France is not like China. In television terms that means if you've arrived with a wonderful anecdote about your mother and some clot asks about your father you reply father's worn out coping with my mother WHO ...You say what you have come to say no matter what.

Resident Alien – The Play

His first TV appearance was judged a success. As a result he started to receive invitations to speak to groups of people 'of varying denominations', as Quentin put it. Some were literary: to these he repeated one of his favourite phrases that 'books were for writing not for reading'. He would elaborate on this saying that if a person had literary ambition he should not read any other works in his chosen category, otherwise he would feel obliged to write 'literature' instead of trying to say what he or she actually meant. This was a lesson he had learned to his cost with his previous literary efforts.

When not with aspirant authors he visited universities or art schools: these he told that education was 'a mistake' and that filling one's head with facts about any subject other than yourself was a complete nonsense.

I would try and get children to see that politics is a complete waste of time and education is a last wild effort on the part of the authorities to prevent an overdose of leisure from driving the world mad. Learning is no longer an improver: it is merely the most expensive time filler the world has ever known. If when you peer into your soul you find that you are ordinary, then ordinary is what you must remain, but you must be so ordinary that you can imagine someone saying 'come to my party and bring your humdrum friend' and everyone knowing that he means you.

Resident Alien – The Play

Whilst there was an element of impishness in his declaration to those in full-time study that education was pointless (he himself was highly self-educated), his assertion that in order to make your mark you had to become more like yourself, even if that meant becoming more 'humdrum', was absolutely earnest. He had learned the hard way that growing up to be yourself is one of the most difficult and treacherous projects a person can embark on.

To art students he took a different line, perhaps because he thought they'd agree with him if he said education was a waste of time. To them he suggested they avoid writing about social issues. Remember, this was 1969 and the young people of the world wanted profoundly to alter the political landscape. He of course believed none of it.

The trouble with politics is it makes children believe that the perpetual violent turmoil of the world is soluble and this means they grow up with this terrible feeling that the world has been mismanaged by their parents, and that they must change it. Therefore they either take jobs where they can opt out entirely: or have the view that they should all go out to the middle of Biafra, and this to my mind is bad. There are situations which cannot be resolved; there are questions for which there are no answers and if you don't accept this then you will rapidly develop a police mentality. You will search for culprits, you will tear up contradictory evidence and you will push people around until they are in easily labelled and easily controlled blocs. Zealots are totally incapable of any emotion other than rage. It is an unalterable law that people who claim to care about the human race are utterly indifferent to the sufferings of individuals.

Resident Alien – The Play

Not surprisingly this didn't always play well with young, politically aware, art students. On one occasion, in East Ham, a young man stormed from the room where Quentin was speaking. He returned a few minutes later telling Quentin he had to leave to cool his rage 'You're lucky,' the student told him. 'I've got a terrible temper and I nearly clobbered you.' Quentin couldn't resist saying the wrong thing at the right time, or the right thing at the wrong time as he doubtless saw it.

Inevitably the groups he was most often asked to address were members of the Campaign For Homosexual Equality or other similar organisations. It seemed to Quentin that at this stage most of these meetings were largely social and, though political, not stridently so. There were trips along the Thames, musical evenings, even a CHE fair. Quentin said that because his sister was the wife of a country parson he was never contemptuous of such occasions. However there was an element he disliked, and this crystallised in his mind during a visit to Bristol. He had been invited there to help declare it a 'gay city'. The convener of the event stood up at the ceremony and said, 'This is a gay week, and I mean GAY. I know the place is full of gay bars and that many of you stand in them night after night but you never speak to anyone, you never seem to be enjoying yourselves.'

Quentin had discovered a soulmate and never tired of repeating such sentiments to the groups he spoke to. Whilst he realised his primary function on such occasions was to entertain, he also warned them of the dangers of forming 'an exile's view of reality'. He said that just because homosexuals were on the outside of certain experiences with 'their cold noses pressed against the window pane' they should not make the mistake of supposing that on the inside all was fine and dandy. Many, Quentin said, 'were on the inside trying to get out'. Whilst many would criticise Quentin for asserting that homosexuality was an 'abnormality' they often forgot that he had no respect for 'normality' either.

It is tempting to think that Quentin was an overnight success; but it is not of course the truth. These forays into the world of public speaking earned him only around £5 a time and a free meal, still not enough on which to survive, let alone transform his life. He was forced to continue modelling, though he was able to do less of it. He was still not in the arena, but he at least had a ringside seat. His friends, and indeed Quentin himself thought that the success of his book may gain him a permanent part in the circus but it had not. His agent came to the rescue.

Love does not cause jealousy

Love does not cause jealousy, it is jealousy that engenders love.

His agent suggested that he wrote another book, on the subject of style. He issued him with a plan for the project, detailing the subjects of each chapter. Quentin was not impressed and felt that the only way to gain the interest of a prospective publisher was to actually write the book.

The longer Quentin thought about the subject the more he said he found he could write about it. He presented it to Jonathan Cape but surprisingly they declined it, and Quentin said he embraced his 'oldest friend defeat'. For a moment he had to contemplate the possibility that his one brief shining moment of success was already behind him. He placed the manuscript under his bed and returned to normal life. However, a few weeks later he received a visit from an actress friend of his who had married into the Woolf family. She asked him wistfully, 'Don't you ever write anything that Cecil might publish?' Quentin dived under the bed and pulled out the manuscript. 'If he doesn't want it,' he said, 'throw it away.' He heard nothing.

A short time later he was approached by Denis Mitchell, 'the famous maker of television documentaries', who asked if he would be interested in becoming the subject of an half-hour *World In Action* piece. On hearing this news Mr Woolf immediately agreed to publish Quentin's book. Thus Quentin learned what he called 'Proust's Law': 'Love does not cause jealousy, it is jealousy that engenders love.' The book that eventually emerged was entitled *How To Have A Life-Style*; with its opening sentence: 'Style is not the man; it is something better. It is a dizzy, dazzling structure that he erects about himself, using as building materials selected elements from his own character' to set the tone for what is, essentially, a witty lecture on the nature of, and the uses and abuses of, style. Early on he offers a memorable definition of what style means to him: 'Style is an idiom arising spontaneously from the personality but deliberately maintained.' One suspects that this definition, as in much of what Quentin states in the book, had grown directly from personal experience. As a child he had learned to endure the mockery of his classmates by exaggerating the very things they found most funny – by embracing his deficiencies fully he had overcome them. Here he tells the reader to do the same.

> *You need to cultivate a lifestyle first for your own benefit – to give you a firm belief in your own identity and to prevent you from importuning others for their approval to make up for your lack of self-esteem*

He goes on to tell them, 'In the end you have only one thing to offer the world that no-one else can give and that is yourself.' The book is a hugely entertaining read in which Quentin discusses everything from 'the nature and projection of style' to 'the rules and standards of style'. His subjects include Mohammad Ali, Mae West, Salvador Dalí and, his old favourite, the great political stylist Eva Perón and he tells us how and why these people are examples of style. Some of what he says is in some ways already covered in *The Naked Civil Servant*. It is almost as if in *How To Have A Life-Style* Quentin is re-visiting his life story and extracting the general principles from the crucial turning points – the teacher imparting the lessons he has learnt.

But, before the book could be published, the documentary had to be made. Initially Quentin was not keen on the idea. He remembered how little he had enjoyed watching others that had been made about similar 'hooligans'. However he gave it the go ahead saying, 'If we wish to be totally free from blame for our anonymity we must never say no to anything.' He met up with a researcher in the As You like It in Soho. Following this, he met Mr Mitchell himself who talked to him at great length and ended the conversation saying, 'I think we'll make it in your room.' 'Make what?' inquired Quentin. 'The film,' replied Mr Mitchell. 'About Soho?' 'No,' said Mr Mitchell. 'It won't be about Soho, it will be about you.'

Early in October 1968 a production team of six arrived at his flat in Beaufort Street. The room itself was unable to accommodate them all and the sound recordists were forced to spend most of their time in the bathroom. Quentin said the net result was the girl who lived in the back room on his floor couldn't go to the lavatory for a week. Not only was the routine of the house disturbed but the whole neighbourhood was affected by the chug of the generator outside the window. Sheets of pink acetate were placed over the windows and Quentin said, 'For four days as though lit by the dawn of a new Doris Day, I walked about, sat on my chair or rolled on my bed droning on about eternal things.' The result was eventually edited down to half an hour and shown at the end of 1969: a remarkable portrait of Quentin, his life and his views. The film took the form of appearing to let Quentin simply talk as he pottered around his room making cups of tea or getting ready. What came across was, again, a picture of a man almost out of Samuel Beckett. When I saw it for the first time, at his memorial service, I was amazed at how similar in format it was to the play I ended up writing. In essence it was the forerunner to his one-man show staged in his own room. What's also interesting is that, even then, he was talking about his readiness for death. Little did he know he had 30 more years to 'endure'.

The documentary gave Quentin his first chance to see his image through the eyes of other people. From here on in he knew what it was they were responding to and he could develop it further. The brand was in place, all it needed was the 'marketing'. The film thrust him into a state of 'semi-fame' and with it phone calls and letters began to arrive from people he had never met.

Immediately after the publication of *The Naked Civil Servant* he had begun to receive phone calls from 'part or total strangers'. Initially these were at the rate of about one a week, along with a similar amount of mail. Quentin wasn't quite sure about this new departure in his life and worried about the kind of people who were attempting to contact him. He asked a friend, 'Have you ever written to anyone you didn't know?' 'Of course I have,' she replied. 'You're much more likely to find you have something in common with someone who's work you admire than with a man who merely happens to be married to your sister.' Whilst appreciating the undeniable logic of her statement Quentin was still not entirely convinced and he treated his correspondents with caution. Many of the letters he received were from women and this was a pattern that would be repeated throughout his life.

> *The other people who write to me are women in middle life and over and over again they ask me the same burning question 'is there life after marriage?' The answer is no. The constant proximity of another person will cramp your style in the end, unless that person is somebody you love and then the burden will become unbearable at once. How can anybody begin each dawn with a fresh assault on his lifestyle if the moment he opens his eyes he hears a voice beside him saying 'and another thing'.*

Resident Alien – The Play

Quentin had a special appeal to middle-aged women. When *Resident Alien* was staged at the Bush I was amazed at how many of our audience were women in 'middle life'. Perhaps there was something in his attitude to co-habitation and housework that really struck a chord or maybe they intuitively keyed in to the strong feminine side of his nature. But Quentin asserted that the only reason most of his correspondence was from women was because men have no time to write letters because they are 'too busy pursuing things which give them pleasure'.

Initially Quentin didn't respond to the letters he received, unless they specifically requested it. His reasoning for this was interesting. He said he thought words were 'the salve with which we heal the wounds inflicted on us by our actions'. He believed, and maintained that he had discovered through his own life, that if an unpleasant incident were recounted with enough regularity its sharp edges would become 'bevelled'. Moreover, he thought that if a problem was recounted with sufficient accuracy 'the solution has in the process already been formulated' and, therefore, no response was really necessary – the writers already knowing in their heart the answer to the question. This exemplifies what I think was ultimately a central part of the Crisp philosophy: his belief that people should take responsibility for their own lives and not seek to blame the world for their ills.

Not surprisingly, he said the question that he was asked the most often was, 'Shall I tell my parents I am gay?' This was seemingly a question which he did answer. He recommended that they neither confirm nor deny it if asked. He warned them, 'Do not say anything that leads them to believe you may be heterosexual.' Loosely speaking: the truth that 'dare not speak it's name'.

Following the broadcast of Mr Mitchell's documentary, Quentin started to receive more phone calls than letters and these were not always friendly calls. As a result Quentin decided that letter writers were 'a restrained race whilst television viewers were a violent people'. Some of the people who called him sought merely to inconvenience him: they would pose as a worker of a television company and invite him to Euston Station to be photographed; or invite him to non-existent interviews in obscure parts of London. At other times efforts were made to embarrass him socially by inviting him to parties where 'there will be lots of lovely young boys'. Quentin was rather baffled: he could have understood these weak attempts at entrapment if the programme had made any secret of his homosexuality but as it made it so patently obvious what could anyone gain 'even if I express ludicrous agreement to attend a kinky orgy'. At other times he said he would receive calls from someone calling themselves 'Nigel' or 'Basil' or some other name the caller throught sounded queer requesting information on what it was like to be homosexual, often saying things like, 'I've never done it myself but I've always wanted to and wouldn't mind if someone did it for me.' Quentin said they must envisage him as 'some doctor figure in rimless glasses and a white coat stood at the top of the stairs and saying "next please".'

However, despite the unfriendliness of some of his calls he made a policy of never berating his attackers and never losing his temper. A friend asked him how he developed this skill and he put it down to the fact that he was the youngest child and consequently had been the butt of mockery and abuse almost from birth. He said he would have 'died of exhaustion' if he had tried to combat the treatment he received. Instead he feigned not to be angry. 'The only method known to me by which one can survive one's emotions is to feign not to have them.' This comment is interesting in that it in some way contradicts his assertion that if you tell yourself you do not feel something you actually stop feeling it. However, it was the same tactic he had deployed on the streets of London when attacked – a policy he called 'other cheekism'. He said it was 'a vital component of every weak person's survival kit'.

It was a skill he would increasingly need as the number of phone calls and letters he was receiving now were as nothing to those that would come following his next foray into the 'arid dust bowl of television'. This next appearance would finally put the name 'Quentin Crisp' on the international map.

Television has so much spare time

Television has so much spare time that everyone will be on it in the end.

Following the broadcast of the *World In Action* documentary, Quentin had set to work in earnest on his *How To Have A Life-Style* book. It was during one such afternoon that he got a phone call from his Publisher, Jonathan Cape. They wanted to know if the movie rights to *The Naked Civil Servant* were for sale. Quentin said that initially he thought the enquiry must be a joke. However, when he discovered the enquiry was from Mr Hagerty he had to take it seriously.

Quentin said Mr Hagerty had been an airman during the War although he didn't seem to fly much and more often than not 'was found with his feet firmly on terra firma in the hooligan cafés of Fitzrovia'. Quentin said he had 'a taste for tall girls which seemed to take up a lot of his time' but occasionally, when not pursuing long-legged beauties, he had joined Quentin and his party for lunch or dinner and Quentin had got to know him slightly. Towards the end of the War he had disappeared. However, now the battles were over, he too had become a member of the documentary film industry.

Quentin immediately called him to ask if his enquiry about the film rights was genuine. He told him that it was and, what's more, brought the name of Philip Mackie into the equation. Mackie was not known to Quentin but would later go on to become famous for writing television dramas. The three met up and had long conversations about the form the film might take. Mackie spent hours taping conversations with Quentin, many of which centred on his sex life and his treatment on the streets of London. From these conversations and a perusal of *The Naked Civil Servant* Mackie produced a scenario. To begin with Quentin was far from impressed. To Quentin the scenario seemed 'fragmented and incomplete'. It was only later he realised that

Mackie had rather wisely omitted the sections of the story which did not contain a strong enough visual element. At this stage, however, that was the least of their worries. Mackie had to find someone to back the movie which at his conservative estimate would cost three quarters of a million pounds to make. Quentin joked that Mr Mackie could get Elizabeth Taylor to play him for that kind of money. Not surprisingly, given the subject matter and the legendary conservativeness of the people who finance movies, Mackie struggled – though there was a moment when an un-named tycoon offered to finance the whole thing so long as the drag artist, Danny La Rue, could be induced to play the part. Quentin said he was delighted with this offer and suggested they turn his story into a musical. Thankfully Mackie declined, and one can't help reflecting how different the rest of this story may have been had he not. However, having declined the offer of La Rue, Mackie was forced to run 'hatless through the streets of London attempting to raise finance' for the film for 'four long years' – but with no success.

After a few months Quentin said he forgot all about the film and went back to work on his lifestyle book which he finished in 1972. But this too turned out to be a 'bomb with a very long fuse' and it did not see the light of day for another three years.

The next few years were a period of stability and little change for Quentin. He was still modelling occasionally and making appearances at various functions to speak. Then, in the summer of 1975, he received a call from his Agent that was to open up a whole new vista.

His Agent had found himself with some money to spare and had decided to spend it by investing in a play at the then fledgling London Fringe Theatre, the King's Head, in Islington. The venue was then as it is today: tiny and cramped and the patrons were forced to perch on stools at small tables as if in some kind of 'Berlin cabaret'. He was renting the venue for the whole period and wanted someone to 'go on' at lunchtimes. He suggested Quentin give a show, 'I thought you could go on then.' Quentin said, 'With what object my good man?' 'You could talk to people.' Quentin asked him what about. His Agent replied that it didn't matter and he needn't say the same thing every day. The man then wisely went off to Spain. And so it was ('alone and totally unprepared' as he put it) that Quentin 'tottered' into the profession of public speaking.

The drama on which his Agent had decided to invest his money was called *Madame De Sade*.

> *Though written by a Japanese gentleman called Mr Mishima about a Frenchwoman it was written on Greek lines. No action took place on stage; the audience was informed what had happened or was warned what was about to happen but it was always elsewhere. Not surprisingly it failed. Not even the presence of Heather Chasen striding up and down in thigh-length boots and carrying a whip as long as Upper Street was enough to satisfy the audiences.*

Quentin said that a contemporary audience far from being satisfied with action taking place off-stage wanted to see a weapon used, 'preferably on the person next to them'. And, at lunchtimes, Quentin went on. Would he fare any better?

The subject on which he had decided to speak was 'lifestyle'. It enabled him to talk to the audience about their own foibles and it also enabled him to mine the wealth of material and anecdote he had prepared whilst writing the book. The performances were not a success. On many occasions the number in the audience was barely more than the number of people actually on the stage, namely one. However, Quentin learned a great deal.

Firstly he realised that his idea of saying different things on each night was impossible. He simply didn't have a broad enough breadth of material. He also discovered, he said, 'That whilst speaking one sentence it was necessary to have some idea of what you were going to say next.' One reviewer said all he did was recite passages from his book in a 'terrible whine'. Whilst being able to use the material from *How To Have A Life-Style* was a godsend in one way it also proved to be a trap as it seduced him into quoting 'the same jokes from the same pages each day and not only that but to moving to the same position on the platform to deliver them'. After three weeks Quentin asked to be spared any further embarrassment and the show was pulled. Luckily however, Philip Mackie, came to the rescue.

My representative on earth

Mr Hurt became my representative on earth.

After four exhausting years attempting to get finance for *The Naked Civil Servant* as a motion picture, and failing, Philip Mackie had persuaded Thames Television to make the piece as a TV movie. Quentin received the call he had long given up hope of ever receiving and a car was quickly dispatched to Beaufort Street to transport him to Teddington Studios. He was amazed by the extravagance of this, up to this point in his life he said he had never earned 'more than £12 a week and had only received £350 for the film rights to *The Naked Civil Servant*'.

At the studios he was introduced to Jack Gold, the Director, and to John Hurt who was to play him and become, what Quentin famously described, as his 'representative on earth'. Hurt immediately said to him, 'I have no intention of merely giving a vaudeville imitation of you.' Quentin saw this occasion as a major turning point in his life. He described it as the 'turning of the tide against which I had been swimming for 60 years'. More than that he was delighted that,

After a lifetime of condemnation for my sexual deviation, that very fact was to be used to present me to the world as being of interest for human reasons that transcended my sin.

However, there were many who thought Hurt mad to play Quentin. John Osbourne, who met Quentin at a party after the film was shown, said that he had ruined Hurt's career and 'made sure that man never gets another good part'. Even Hurt's Agent thought he shouldn't do it. Hurt was unperturbed. I asked Gold why he thought Hurt refused to give in and Gold said, 'He's an actor, I think he recognised a cracking good part in a terrific screenplay. It was the best screenplay I ever received.'

Quentin was engaged as a technical advisor and this enabled him to be paid while on location. He visited just four of them. Firstly he saw the scene from the opening of the film where he dances in front of a mirror as a young child in a dress. Later in the day he was taken to Richmond and then, finally, he visited a café and an art school class. It was only here that he offered any advice as he feared Hurt may not know what it was like to actually be an art school model. He needn't have worried, Hurt had been an art student as a young man. Quentin was amazed by the intensity with which the whole production team cared about the project and about whether it accurately represented his life or not. The art department took pictures of him from all angles and they took him to a shop in Burlington Street so that the wig maker would be able to 'reconstruct the architecture' of his hair. In the end they made five wigs so that Hurt could pass from 'innocence (scarlet) to senility (discreet mauve)'. Whilst the whole thing was shot in just 21 days, Gold said he thought everyone was aware of how important it was to get it right, not just for the sake of the drama but for the sake of a whole section of society that it would implicitly be representing. Interestingly, Gold maintained that although he thought the film may cause 'a bit of a fuss' his reason for doing it was because it was 'a great screenplay'. Perhaps this was one of the reasons for its success, the film's agenda was implied and not stated. Though it became seen as a campaigning film it was not conceived as one. The dramatic imperatives of good character and story and dialogue remained firmly at the top of the shopping list of its creators.

Interestingly, despite being used extensively by the producers in order to enable Hurt to achieve the same physical likeness, Quentin maintained that he spent little or no time with Hurt to advise him on playing the part – though Gold's recollections are slightly different and he recalls that Hurt and Quentin did at least enjoy a dinner together. Despite this Quentin said Hurt 'included in his characterisation all sorts of tiny details'. Though on location Quentin had offered little directly, Hurt had observed and inwardly digested much indirectly and as a result was able to avoid the trap of playing him, as Quentin described, a 'camp scarecrow' and instead reveal Quentin as, in his own words, 'a helpless victim of a misguided dream'. In truth the film was much more complex than that. Gold said he thought that what Hurt captured was 'a man who had no hypocrisy, no deception, no pretence'.

When the film was finally finished Quentin was invited to a preview screening where it was shown to the press. A car arrived at Beaufort Street and took him to the Thames' studios in Euston Road. The car was late and as a consequence he missed the opening. Quentin was very worried because he knew that afterwards the press would want to know what he thought, so in the car on the way he prepared an answer. When questioned he said that the film of his life had been much better than the real thing because 'it was much shorter'. Quentin said later that he had great difficulty viewing the piece with any degree of objectivity and in typical fashion said that it was the kind of programme that, had he not been involved in it, he would never have watched in a million years as he said he had 'long since ceased to be interested in the subject of homosexuality' believing there was nothing fresh to be said about the topic.

In spite of this assertion Quentin was well aware that an excellent piece had been produced. Hurt managed to capture the charm and the danger and the style of Quentin without ever slipping into parody, and Philip Mackie's screenplay captured the full horror of the treatment Quentin received on the streets of London without ever allowing the film to slip into the niche of victim portrayal as so many of the gay films that came before it had done. There were many memorable moments, including the famous dream sequence in Portsmouth in which Quentin is surrounded by beautiful sailors in crisp, white uniforms. The Television Critic, David Aaronivitch, said recently it was the first time he recalled seeing a television portrayal of homosexuality which actually made you think, 'I wonder if I'd have had more fun if I'd been gay?' (In a recent poll the sequence ranked at number 69 in a poll of people's all time top-100 TV moments.) Interestingly Gold would confess to me later that the only reason it was shot as a fantasy in the studio was because the budget was running out and they were terrified that the weather would let them down on location.

The film was first shown to the public in 1977 and it was an instant hit. Gold said that all concerned were extremely worried about the public reaction but in the event the film received 'no condemnation and much commendation'. In those 'Halcyon days', before the advent of satellite TV or Channels 4 and 5 it was possible for a TV play to get the whole nation talking and *The Naked Civil Servant* had done just that. On the day after it was shown Quentin was walking through Shepherd's Bush when a lorry stopped and the driver wound down the window of his cab and asked if he was Quentin Crisp. Quentin nervously admitted he was and the driver said 'homosexuality and that, I gettit now' before driving off.

The critics were almost unanimous in their praise and much of the glory fell on the shoulders of Quentin. Clive James said that Quentin was 'some kind of hero'. Quentin had been convinced that some critics would focus on the 'depravity' in his life story, if it really existed, but no mention was made of this. They had taken his story at face value and understood the unspoken heroism contained within. Nancy Banks-Smith wrote that the piece was so strong and so important that it 'justified the existence of television itself'. It was to change his life.

His Agent said, 'From now on you must accept the fact that you will become part of the fantasies of total strangers.' But even that couldn't have prepared him for what was to come. As Quentin said,

> *Previously when people had been asked in surveys on the subject of homosexuality what a homosexual looked like they would say (if they had never met one) that they wore bright colours and behaved in an 'actorish' way. Now they said 'oh, you know, like Quentin Crisp'.*

His name became synonymous with homosexuality itself: the cause now had a spokesman. However he had never sought to be the spokesman for anything other than himself – as they were quick to discover.

The day after the broadcast Quentin was interviewed on daytime television by Mavis Nicholson who was then the queen of the genre. Following his first appearance on TV he had taken to watching chat shows in an attempt to learn the techniques needed. He decided that the key was to find a way of talking intimately with the interviewer whilst remembering that both of them were on show to a large number of people. He also realised that you had to be aware of the nature of your audience and that 'to talk about the great difficulties of writing books in front of people who had to get up every day at 4 a.m. to go to the factory or deliver the milk' was not a good way to win friends or influence people. Also, perhaps most importantly, he realised that the first law of television is to 'say what you have come to say, no matter what'. He did.

Months earlier Miss Nicholson had interviewed two men in a very serious atmosphere and asked them if it was true that gay men found forming lasting relationships very difficult. They said 'yes' but lay the blame firmly at the door of intolerance that did so much to drive gay people apart and to legitimise only heterosexual relations. Quentin had seen this interview and regretted the fact that neither of them had said they were glad they couldn't form lasting relationships as it freed them from the 'damp, dark prison of eternal love'. Miss Nicholson must have read this quote from Quentin because she repeated it to him and he was happy to confirm it. His mischievous, witty persona and his refusal to toe the party line made him an instant success. At one point Quentin mentioned the word camp and then followed it by looking directly at the camera and saying, 'Do you think your little friends will understand the word?' Miss Nicholson leaned forward and gave the lens a searching look herself before adding, 'I should think so.' The chemistry between the two worked and the interview was a triumph. Whilst his first TV appearance on *Late Night Line Up* had gone well Quentin felt he had only given the right answers to the questions and 'not put much of himself into the appearance'. This time he had vowed to add what he was to what he said. He had succeeded.

Clearly, whilst Quentin would have made far more money out of *The Naked Civil Servant* had it been made as a cinema film the fact that it was made for television ultimately gave it far more impact in Quentin's eyes. In those days, and indeed to some extent in these days, if a film has a homosexual content

Quentin said 'it quickly becomes advertised directly or indirectly for the fact and it attracts only an audience of people who are either gay, or liberal or wish to be seen as so'.

On television the film reached a hugely mixed audience in the way that television often reaches people, by default, and Quentin loved to tell the story of the middle-class couple he imagined watching it. The wife in the kitchen washing up, the husband flicking through the TV pages:

Wife:	*What's on channel 1?'*
Husband:	*A documentary.*
Wife:	*What's on the other side?*
Husband:	*The queers*
Wife:	*Let's watch that.*

Quentin knew that though television sought to be a window on the whole world the small screen loved abnormality above all else.

The net result was that complete strangers started to speak to Quentin in the street. Whereas previously following the documentary people had been wary, now having seen his life acted out and having read critics praising him for it they were much less hostile: the small screen had legitimised his 'abnormality'. The same, however, could not now be said of the letter writers and telephone callers. Some of the calls he began to receive were very strange indeed. On one occasion the police arrived having received information that a lesbian was planning to kill him. The attack never materialised. He was not just under attack from the enemy, those on his own side were far from happy.

Whilst Quentin's identity had remained only in the written word the gay movement accepted and, to some extent, welcomed him, though *Gay News* expressed the opinion that 'it would have been better for the cause if *The Naked Civil Servant* had been published posthumously', which Quentin described as a literary way of saying 'drop dead'. However now with the film and his increasing appearances on television he was moving from idea to icon and, as he put it, his 'struggle to ingratiate himself with the majorities grew horribly apparent'.

He was invited to address all the homosexuals in Westminster, 'the postal district not the Houses of Parliament' and he was roundly attacked, including someone who accused Quentin of once being the Martin Luther King of the movement but who had now become someone who spent his time expressing 'Uncle Tom' sentiments. Quentin explained that he was never militant but that his actions were merely local. They were not impressed, he simply wouldn't toe the line. The new image of gayness was 'ordinariness'. Homosexuals were appearing regularly on TV saying just how normal they were, just how like everyone else. Quentin was not impressed, saying that 'only in Illinois would the ploy of advertising your ordinariness ingratiate you with the populace'. To Quentin the idea of group identity was anathema. After a lifetime spent trying to be recognised for who he was and accepted and ultimately loved for the fact that he was different, the idea of submerging himself in group identity was abhorrent. He believed that the kind of people who joined such groups and went on such marches were often the ones most lacking an individual voice.

The trouble with this method of trying to gain more liberty is that those who adopt it, instead of bowing to the laws of the community in general must conform to the narrower and even less rewarding constraints of their chosen regiment.

Uniform looks were now entering the gay lexicon – tractor boots, blue jeans, builder's shirts – and Quentin deplored this new fashionable 'ghetto'.

I have never liked ghettos. I once met a man at an airport who said that the homosexuals of Minnesota are in favour of the 'separate-but-equal' solution to their problems. I said 'why?' He said 'we don't have anything in common with the straights'. What a peculiar thing to say. They have everything in common except their funny way of spending their evenings. If you only talk about your sex life you will never have anything in common with anyone. And this man's 'constant companion' recalled that I had once declared that if Mr Clinton announced that he was converting Indiana into a reservation for homosexual people and that we must all go and live there I would burst into tears. I still think that. I would feel I was

being starved of reality. If I think about my life I see it as a slow journey from the
outer suburbs of ostracism almost to the heart of the world – assuming it has
a heart. I would not wish to be shunted into a siding. The trouble with gay
reservations is they breed a terrible uniformity. They claim to be a place where
people can be themselves but very often that involves the most boring form of camp
which has nothing to do with individual style and everything to do with the fear
of 'breaking ranks'.

Resident Alien – The Play

Whilst it is easier to sympathise with Quentin's views now, in an age of
greater tolerance and in which some of the battles have been won, it is easy to
understand why the more radical gays of the time felt Quentin to be a
reactionary force. He refused however to give in, declaring that he felt the net
result of too much stridency was maybe that less, not more, tolerance would
be given to homosexuality. However his cry to avoid replacing one type of
uniformity (the straight world) with another (the gay world) was absolutely
apposite, though few wanted to hear it.

Where did these reactions come from? At least in part they came from his
profoundly conservative up bringing and the fact that he was two generations
away from many of the young people at the forefront of the gay movement. It
is easy to forget that by now he was well into his seventh decade on earth and
had been born an Edwardian. However I think, more importantly, they
emerged from a refusal to go back to a state of ostracism he had lived so long
in. He had spent almost 60 years trying to escape the ghetto of 'normality' and
could not face entering another ghetto. Whilst he found strength in the gay
world he did not wish to live there solely. Many of his old friends and, more
importantly, many of his new ones were straight people. He said, 'I represent
no-one other than my puny self.'

That puny self was by now famous. He returned to the King's Head pub to
have a second attempt at 'the public speaking racket'.

I've gone into the fame business

I've gone into the fame business, people say to me 'you can't just do fame',
but I can.

His second attempt on the summit of public speaking was very different from
the first. When he had last appeared the audience was often outnumbered by
ushers. Now, following the television broadcast of *The Naked Civil Servant,* it
was a very different story. 'The little group of supportive friends had been
replaced by a full house of strangers.' And society figures too were latching
onto Quentin's turn. One lunchtime Lady Diana Cooper came with Mrs
Churchill. Quentin said she wore a huge black hat 'as though she were in
mourning for Ascot'. This time his appearance was a great success.

Quentin was still not entirely convinced he had cracked it though. Secretly he
suspected that the audience who 'nipped out of the office during their lunch
hour for a quick show, a pint and a pie' had lower expectations than those
who booked tickets, employed babysitters and ventured out into the cold
London night to see a fully fledged evening show. He made a mental note to
address this problem at some point.

But first he was to make his debut performance at the Edinburgh Festival. He
went there in the autumn of 1976. In the madcap atmosphere of Edinburgh
he had a great time. He was working for a group of students from Bristol
University. He appeared at the Heriot-Watt Theatre. On his first performance
he concluded his act by asking the audience if they had understood and,
furthermore, believed him. A man sitting at the back of the house complained
that he had not, as he had hoped, conducted 'a serious existential discussion'.
Quentin apologised and said that just because he was smiling 'he should not
think that I did not at any time say what I did not mean'. Alongside the man
was his wife who said in response to an earlier comment, 'Why is it not

possible for me to have a lifestyle if I have children?' Quentin replied that 'the trouble with children is they are not returnable' (of course a line plundered from his autobiography). The audience laughed uproariously at this remark at which point the man switched his attack to the audience itself accusing them all of all being 'sycophants'. He carried on but his enemies took no notice of him and Quentin claimed in this moment to fully understand what Ingrid Bergman had said in her autobiography that 'people came to the theatre hoping to be entertained and not to be informed'. Quentin later regretted the incident and said he should have dealt with it in a totally different way, inviting the speaker onto the stage where they could have conducted 'a reasoned debate which would have added to the show itself'. He was learning fast.

During his run in Edinburgh he was 'summoned back' to London by Thames Television so that he might appear on a programme with John Hurt and Mary Whitehouse, self-styled chairman of the National Viewers and Listeners Campaign, a movement against sex and violence and bad language and other assorted sinning on television and radio. The show was compared by Mr Cavett. In typical Quentin style he said he admired Mrs Whitehouse, though 'wasn't sure that his adulation was something the lady sought'. Quentin said Mrs Whitehouse 'knew exactly what she was doing and just as Germaine Greer uses self-doubt to soften her personality Mrs Whitehouse adds to her puritanical image a pinch of sensuality'. She did this, according to Quentin, by choosing 'an outfit which ran slightly counter to her image, thus confusing the audience and preventing them from accusing her of being a dull dried-up old stick'. Interestingly when asked if she had found *The Naked Civil Servant* shocking she replied that she had not, and added that she thought the programme had been sympathetically made and she had 'learned a great deal'.

After the show Mr Cavett said that if Quentin ever went to the States he would have him on his show. Quentin laughed – at this point it still seemed the remotest of possibilities.

When his Edinburgh run had ended he returned to London only to discover his Agent had booked him to appear at a small theatre called the New End

Theatre in Hampstead for a two-week run, this time in the evening. Here was the opportunity Quentin had waited for to find out if he would get as good a response in the evenings as he had done to his lunchtime show at the King's Head. It also posed a more immediate problem: Quentin had only enough material for half of the evening, his previous incarnation of the show having lasted just an hour. His Agent came up with a solution suggesting that before the interval Quentin should ask members of the audience to write questions down on pieces of paper which Quentin would then answer in the second half. The show was thus divided into two equal halves which lasted in all about two and a quarter hours.

It worked a treat. The audience, able to file their questions anonymously, lost their inhibitions and when Quentin answered them other audience members shouted their own responses. It gave him a solid framework for the second half and enabled him to introduce a greater spontaneity into the show. The first half of the evening still bore the hallmarks of being culled from his books but he said 'the colour' was able to return to his voice in the second half. He now had a whole evening's entertainment and had found the format for the show *An Evening with Quentin Crisp* which he would perform all over the world right up until his death. The show would begin with the words:

Good evening, I have been forbidden to say this is a straight talk from a bent speaker. Instead I shall describe it as a consultation with a doctor who is more ill than you are. I am here to cure you of your freedom because I am sure that it is an excess of freedom that makes the world so unhappy. People have got all this freedom and yet wherever I look people are not rejoicing they are complaining, protesting, in fact throughout the world protest has become the number one game that any number can play. Recently one weekend in London a friend of mine got into the wrong march. That shows you what's going on there. What has made everyone suddenly so angry is the element which has been added to their lives in recent times – their freedom. I know it's too late to ask them to abide by laws handed down by their pastors and masters and elders and betters but what we need are chains. Chains of our own making. However heavy these may be they will never feel as irksome as limitations placed on us by others. Not any old chains – we have to have a system and that begins with each of us trying to decide what it is that makes him the way he is. It involves a journey to the interior – not an altogether pleasant experience because as well as totting up what you consider to be your assets you also have to take a long look at what your friends call 'the trouble with you' and the synthesis between these two opposite opinions will be your identity. You have to polish up your raw identity until it becomes a lifestyle. Something interesting by which you are proud to be identified and something with which you can do barter with the outer world to get from it what you want. I won't say what you deserve because if we all got what we deserve we would starve.

He would quote examples from life of people who demonstrated his thesis. For instance, he asserted that in order to achieve fame you didn't need talent. In order to prove this he invoked the spirit of Sarah Bernhardt.

Now I never saw Sarah Bernhardt on the stage but I have seen a strip of movie showing her coming into the home stretch in Camille. The death scene. She sits opposite Armand on a chaise longue wearing a minimum risk nightdress, with clowns make-up and her hair is right down into her eyes. Now someone must have told her it was a silent movie, but did she care? No, once the cameras started to turn her lips started moving faster than those of a policeman giving corrupt evidence and when her lips moved her eyes began to roll and when her eyes moved a hand shot out into the hair returning later to give her a terrible blow on the chest. Sometimes it was one arm, sometimes it was another, sometimes it was both arms together and then as abruptly as all this activity had began it stopped. Her arm swung down in front of the couch like the limb of a rag doll. Now I am not just trying to foist on you my own Philistine reactions. This movie was shown at the National Film Theatre in London and that is a building to which no-one can obtain admission unless he can prove that he comes from the cheese and wine belts of England but it made no difference. The audience choked with derisive mirth, a man near me fell out into the gangway his feet twiddling in the air. 'La Divine' indeed, it wasn't her acting that made Miss Bernhardt divine, it was her nerve.

Quentin both relished and satirised the notion of being famous for being famous. It was a theme he returned to time and time again. I think there was a part of him that believed he too had achieved this, and there was also the devil in him which knew that this relatively recent phenomenon in some ways challenged the regimented class structure that had shackled him. No longer were all the people on television the product of Oxbridge education, indeed some had no education at all. He extended his thesis to also cover the notion of virtue.

Nowadays you don't even need virtue to have a lifestyle, you no longer have to be an object of public veneration or even affection, you can be the focus of contempt or even downright hatred. After all as a test of whether you are still in touch with someone else, being loved can never be a patch on being murdered. That's when someone really has risked his life for you. And if you decide on depravity as the fluid in which you will suspend your monstrous ego then you have the most wonderful examples behind you. In Medieval France, living at the same time as Joan of Arc there was a great French nobleman called Gilles De Rais and he murdered 150 choirboys in a lifetime. Now quantity is not style. All the same it's difficult not to be impressed isn't it? When he was caught he brought off an effect which I wouldn't advise any of you to attempt if you are just beginners. He reversed his style. Now before you can do this you must be absolutely sure that the image you are taking up is more blinding that the one that you've abandoned. On the first day of his trial he was his usual imperious self, refusing to take any notice of what his accusers told him on the grounds that they were not his equals. On the second day he repented, he confessed so long, so loud, so much, that the bishop who was trying his case rose and covered with a cloth the face of the crucifix hanging on the courtroom wall. Now I tell you this only to show you that style begets style. It means that when you have completed your image of yourself you won't be surrounded by receivers of the news. Your style will magnetise towards you other stylists and you will be able to enjoy them and yourself. Finally when he was condemned to death De Rais cried out 'I am redeemable!' And this brought people from far and wide throughout France to prey for his soul. Now if this is not style it is at least gesture on a national scale all brought about by one man.

How To Have A Life-Style

One writer asserted recently that Quentin was a philosopher constantly being upstaged by a stand-up comic and in his thesis on De Rais both Quentins are very much in evidence. As they are in another passage from *How To Have A*

Life-Style, which would also feature in his one-man show.

But of course before you can build some dizzying, dazzling structure as a monument to yourself you must first get the foundations of your private life absolutely solid. From now on you should have nothing at home that doesn't represent the kind of person you have decided to become. It doesn't matter if your house is full of gadgets which are advertised on TV every 20 minutes – they've got to go. And when you've got rid of the superfluous things you start on the superfluous action. From now onward there should be no doodling and dawdling and I used to say there must be no daydreaming but I've changed my opinion recently. I think you are allowed your daydreams up to the age of 25, but after that they may become an alibi. Do you understand me? It's no good running a pig farm badly for 30 years, whilst saying really I was meant to be a ballet dancer, by that time pigs will be your style. And it follows logically if there's to be no doodling and dawdling there's to be no evening classes. It's alright if you are learning to sing or dance because these are activities the results of which you take out into the world and wear like a crown. People who have learned to sing will always have richer, rounder voices. People who've learned to dance will always have bigger bolder movements, but as for pottery and basket weaving, what good are they? The moment the doors of the evening institute clang shut behind you you are back where you started. On the way home you might get into an argument with a stranger at a bus stop. It's no good saying I can't express myself you"l have to come and see my baskets.

Quentin's pig farm analogy, whilst undoubtably funny, does contain a strong philosophical truth. However, by the time he gets onto his evening class evidence the stand-up comic is very much to the fore, as it is on the subject of Henry Moore:

Of course it's not enough merely to get the foundations of your life in order. You also have to decide what you are going to do in the outer world. Now some of you may be so old-fashioned that you still have jobs. If this is so try not to get stuck in work where you only deal with things, and I include the highest level of things; sculpture, books, paintings they are only objects just like washing machines but not so useful. It would be difficult to express the dilemma that lies before the visual artist. If I showed you a huge great piece of concrete with a hole in it everybody would say it's a Henry Moore, but if I could show you Henry Moore himself nobody would know who he was. So all that clipping, all that chipping, all that chiselling, it's been in vain.

However, by the time he gets onto the subject of equality there is little doubt that the philosopher Quentin again takes hold of the reins:

The difficulty with establishing all this for yourself is we live in a world riddled with envy. People are always squeaking for equality. Equality is a dead word. Never desire to be anyone's equal. Once you have entered the profession of being you have become a professor of a subject about which you are the only living authority. What other people do with their lives, with their style will not matter. Every morning say to yourself, preferably aloud, 'Other people are a mistake!' No I withdraw that remark it might be thought sweeping. Say to yourself, 'Concern with other people is a mistake.' Now I know this is not what most people teach you but I am trying to spare you the traditional scramble for mutual self-sacrifice. Altruism is a debilitating, fragmenting process but the constant watch over and the perfection of your idea of yourself and the presentation of it gift wrapped to others is a unifying and invigorating way of life and it carries with it a built in invitation to the party at the end of the world, that glittering function at which everybody will be speaking but no-one will be listening. If you are armed with your style you will be able to run towards that happy hubbub without the faintest fear that you will be out of your depth. More important the burdens of your sorrowful and angry freedom, these problems of who to be and where to go and even what to think they will fall away from you forever. Do not be the kind of person for whom the band is always playing in the other room. Develop a lifestyle. … Ask yourself, 'If there were no praise, and no blame, who would I be then?' Then you know who you are, and what your style is.

The last phrase is truly one of Quentin's most thrilling and terrifying ideas. It invokes the notion of complete autonomy and invites the reader to stand apart from circumstance and society, instead believing totally in the self. His assertion that altruism is a debilitating way of life is a deliberate provocation to a society brought up on Christian notions. Yet again he was spiking his listeners' witty cocktail with uncomfortable ideas. He deployed a similar tactic with his audiences' heroes. Oscar Wilde, of course, came in for a particular hammering:

Oscar Wilde said in matters of great importance it is not sincerity that matters, but style, yet to me they are the same thing. Style is not a lot of dandyism or flourishes encrusted on your public image. It's a way of stripping yourself of everything but your true self so you can only judge the style by the content and you only reach the content through the style. As far as I'm concerned, people are always saying to me 'all you want to be is noticed'. It isn't enough. I want to be recognised. My appearance is simply a leaflet thrust into the hands of astonished bystanders and this is the reason I think Mr Wilde fell apart.

Quentin clearly doubted Wilde's sincerity and felt that his style was an invention rather than the real man. This is odd given that Quentin Crisp was himself an invention and that he openly admits he taught himself to speak and write in the way he did. I suspect that, in Wilde, Quentin saw much of himself and like all offspring was keen to distance himself as far as possible from the person who in part created him. Without Wilde it is hard to believe that Quentin could have written or spoken in quite the way he did.

To Quentin speaking was everything, and he lived to talk to others, which is why he would rail against the 'curse' of music saying it was the 'maximum amount of noise conveying the minimal meaning'.

Music is a mistake. When I was young the world was silent. Well there were concerts but these took place in concert halls. Now a concert hall is like the Gents, if you feel a certain need you go to the place and there you meet other people in the same predicament and if the place is properly constructed the stench of culture does not seep out into the street. But this is no longer the case. Music is everywhere. One cannot help asking of what were you afraid. Why can't you bare the sound of the puff-puffs on the station, why did you have to have the music? Why couldn't you bare the sound of the barber's clippers? Why have you reduced all human experience to one experience. The music. You've taken away all the variety that there used to be in life. And worse than that you've had to give up the speech.

There is no point in trying to speak and when you give up the words you give up the thoughts. In the beginning there was the word and the word prompts thought. It's when you realise that there are words like greedy, materialistic, avaricious and so on you start to find ideas which express ideas which express these shades of meaning. With music we can only gibber and twitch. One of the great adjuncts of style is vocabulary.

Quentin had an unconventional speaking voice and in many ways it should not have been suited to public performance given how tonally monotonous it could be, but there was something in the care he took to construct his sentences and in the almost ornate quality of his speech patterns that transfixed the listener. Similarly his writing, like Wilde before him, had a voice so clear and distinctive that one can instantly pastiche it. Like Wilde, the essence of the man filled his every nuance. As his great niece, Michele Crawford, said, 'You didn't have a conventional conversation with Quentin.' Instead you were treated to a lesson in style, it was almost as if language was too important to him to be allowed to become merely commonplace. In his early life Quentin had used language time and time again as a means of defending himself from a hostile society, he understood how powerful a tool it could be and relished any opportunity to exercise his power over it.

The essential message of Quentin's show however was one of self-improvement – of becoming more like yourself. He told his audiences that the key was existentialism and defined an existentialist as 'someone who realises he can only exercise his freedom by swimming with the tide but faster'. It was the essence of the tactics he had deployed throughout his life. He had converted his way of living into a philosophy and by his own admission with a little borrowing from many of the great philosophies of the world which he said he had 'domesticated' turned it into entertainment.

The show ran for just two weeks but was a huge success. (Not successful enough to prevent the theatre closing down on Quentin's departure though – a fact that amused him greatly.) However the two weeks in Hampstead were just the beginning of a much longer run of the show. Richard Jackson, Quentin's Promoter and the man who would eventually direct Quentin's

London memorial at the Drill Hall, had been alerted to the fact that a thriller which had been playing at the Duke of York's Theatre on St Martin's Lane in the West End had been pulled off early after very bad notices. He dispatched Quentin off to see the Theatre Manager, Brian Rix, then famous for his bedroom farces at the Whitehall. Typically, Quentin said he did not recognise Mr Rix 'with his trousers up'.

Mr Rix asked Quentin how many people he had played to in Edinburgh. Quentin replied 'about 250 a night'. Mr Rix was relieved, and he asked him what the first thing was he said to them. Quentin said he used to tell his audience that he was 'about to deliver a straight talk from a bent speaker' but that someone had objected to this on the grounds that it gave homosexuality a bad name. Mr Rix looked puzzled, 'So what do you say to them now?' 'I say that I have been forbidden to say that this is a straight talk from a bent speaker.' He got the job.

An Evening With Quentin Crisp opened in January 1978. It was an instant success and the reviews were good. However there was a slight problem when someone from the actors' union, Equity, discovered Quentin was not a member. A deputation was dispatched to Mr Rix's office to ask why he was employing someone who was not a member of the union. Mr Rix swiftly replied that Quentin was 'not acting, he was very sincere'. Though funny the answer did not suffice and Quentin was forced to become a member of the union. During the run at the Duke of York's he developed the performance further. One night early on in the run a gentleman spoke from the audience and asked Quentin if he could prevent the crowd from laughing too soon as he was a little hard of hearing. Quentin said that up to this point he had delivered every line as if it was a joke thinking that this was necessarily what the audience wanted. Now he realised it was not enough just to amuse an audience, he had to also control it.

Another key lesson came from Elaine Strich, all be it by a rather roundabout route. She was convalescing in a hospital bed and rather depressed. Her Agent asked her if there was anything they could get her that would cheer her up. Perhaps half jokingly she said, 'Yeah, get me Quentin Crisp.' The Agent duly obliged and Quentin was dispatched to her bedside. Still troubled by the issue of whether or not to control his audience Quentin asked Miss Strich whether what other actors had said about controlling the audience was true. Her response was typically forthright: 'Don't bother with all that, just get them to like you.' From then on Quentin said he deployed what he called 'Strich's First Law' to his entire life. He later said he took it a stage further and got them to feel sorry for him. Though, he didn't always succeed.

Whilst the show was a hit with large numbers of the straight audience, some members of the gay community were less keen. Quentin said, 'They could not get it in their heads that I am not someone who hires halls throughout the land in order to deliver a manifesto.' It was true that Quentin never mentioned homosexuality unless, in the second half of the programme, he was asked about it. He said he was aware that it was a subject certain members of the audience did not wish to discuss. He was fond of telling the story of how during one show's question-and-answer session a woman asked a question about lesbianism to which Quentin made a reply and then she replied again, before a gentleman in the audience piped up, 'Can't we move onto something of more general interest?'

During the interval of one show he was autographing books in the auditorium when a young man came up angrily and accused him of reading from a script. Quentin denied this but the man retorted that he was and said he was reading from *How To Have A Life-Style*. Quentin said he was making use of it but not quoting word for word. The man was still not happy, 'There are a lot of gay people here tonight and we are waiting for you to tell the audience you're gay.' Quentin was unable to hide his amusement, 'How could that possibly be necessary. What do you think brings people here except that I am the subject of *The Naked Civil Servant*?' The man was still not happy so Quentin suggested he write down a question that would elicit from him 'his guilty secret'. He did so. When Quentin opened his question it said: 'Are you an active or passive homosexual or are you just acting?' Quentin said that 'if he meant by acting, he meant pretending to be someone else then he was not acting'. He went on to explain that by nature he was a passive human being but, 'if the asker of the question was curious about his sexual techniques he could rest assured that in a very long lifetime he had probably done everything he could imagine'. The man was still not impressed. Quentin said, 'He could not help reflecting sadly on the fact that when at last straight people of the world were willing to drop the subject of my long dead sex life, gay people could not leave it alone.' In many ways to a 21st-century readership Quentin was way ahead of the times, wishing to be seen as a whole person and an artist rather than simply a gay one. However, it is also easy to understand the annoyance of the gay rights' lobby who saw in him a potential hero figure but found him, yet again, steadfastly refusing to represent anyone other than his 'puny self'.

This 'puny self' was quite enough for the celebrity audience of London, however, and many of Britain's finest now flocked to hear him speak. Amongst them was the playwright Harold Pinter and his wife Antonia Fraser. They took him to dinner and some time later Pinter came to visit Quentin at Beaufort Street. At the time Quentin was attempting to get an Arts Council Grant and Pinter offered to help him with the application. Some time later he invited Quentin to a party at his colossal house in Hanover Terrace. Quentin said he was

... dazzled by the splendour of the way in which successful dramatists live. If, as the critics at the time asserted, playwrights were preoccupied with their kitchen sinks, they must have been of solid gold.

Always an acute observer of people Quentin said,

Mr Pinter presents to the world a brooding, almost stern aspect. With few facial movements and no gestures of the hands, he gives the impression of stillness and great density of character. It is possible to imagine situations in which he is implacable, even unreasonably so but to me he has always been more than polite. I think by a muted chivalry towards the weak.

Pinter would later say in an interview that, 'The great question with Quentin is, is he lonely?' It was a question that anyone who encoutered the man found hard not to ask. After a run at the Duke of York's the show transferred to the smaller Ambassadors Theatre in West Street, before finally ending its run after eleven weeks. When he left the Stage Door Keeper at the Ambassadors said, 'You'll come back won't you – you could be a one-man "Mousetrap".' It was a comment which always amused Quentin greatly.

Following the West End there was the inevitable provincial tour taking in everywhere from Bury St Edmunds to Mold where Crisp found a whole new audience, many of them middle-aged women who had found in *The Naked Civil Servant* an unlikely hero. Quentin Crisp was very much a national treasure, our very own 'stately homo'.

I don't believe in abroad

I don't believe in abroad. I think they speak English behind our backs.

For many years Quentin had delighted in saying he didn't believe in abroad but following his West End debut an invite to Canada forced him to face up to the fact that it existed.

The Naked Civil Servant had been shown on Canadian television and they wanted him to go and speak about it, all be it just for the day. Quentin was not worried about travelling such a huge distance for a 24-hour visit. He told people he didn't believe in jet lag, especially if journeying from West to East. 'All the plane has to do,' he said, 'is go up into the air and, like Nijinksy, pause there a little; and the destination will come by presently.' The only lag he said he believed in was 'gin lag'. However, even though the distance and time zones didn't worry him there was still the problem of leaving his 'day job': amazingly he was still employed by a number of art schools.

After a few phone calls he managed to extricate himself from his art school posing duties and he boarded his first long-distance flight. He was instantly impressed with the service and the cabin staff who he said 'acted out the delicacies on their trolleys' if you weren't sure what to eat. It was a massive contrast to 'the slaves' employed by British Rail who had previously served him on his British speaking engagements. In other respects he said he found air travel less exciting than the movies had led him to expect.

No-one became hysterical, no-one near me was handcuffed to anyone else and I couldn't nervously glance at the ice forming on the wings because I couldn't see the wings. You eat, you sleep and you go to the movies. You're hardly any better off than on earth.

Yet again Quentin couldn't resist contrasting reality with the movies. It wasn't that it surprised him that real life didn't quite match up to the silver screen, rather that he delighted in making the existentialist point that the order, meaning and conflict imposed by the dramatic imperative in movies is fallacious. He knew as well as anyone that causal logic, however satisfying, was a million miles removed from the actual business of living.

That said, as the plane flew into Toronto Quentin became very excited. The coastline with its innumerable capes, inlets, islands and tiny lakes; the honey-coloured skyscrapers that seemed to rise out of the lake; the secular minaret in the centre of the town which at the time was the largest free-standing building in the world: it was a whole new world. He arrived in North America on the day celebrated as Columbus Day in the States, which he said was highly appropriate as the way he talked about his visit subsequently gave the impression that 'no-one had been there except me and Chris'.

Appropriately having entered this 'New World' the man who was sent to meet him at the airport was a certain Mr Dvorak who escorted him in a gleaming black limousine to the great glass Toronto Hotel where Quentin couldn't resist standing outside and looking at his reflection in the 'identity parade glass' from which the building was made. It enabled him to view himself with the words 'Toronto Hotel' written backwards above his head. He really was here.

There was not much time for thought though because, before he even had had a chance to properly unpack his case, he received a call from the paperback publisher of *The Naked Civil Servant* who had a list of radio stations he wished him to visit the following day. Previously this would have worried him, but he was now getting into his stride with the fame game. He did four interviews in quick succession, in between he managed a visit to a newspaper called *Body Politic*, the gay voice of Toronto. Quentin said the paper featured a front-page story about a man who had been dismissed from his job as a horse trainer because he was gay. (Quentin said it was 'difficult to imagine what goes on in the minds of some heterosexuals'.) He said he thought the people who ran the paper were disappointed that he wasn't more strident. After the

129 Beaufort Street,
LONDON S. W. 3.
FLAxman 9398

17th. May '78

Your last letter,
                dear Mrs. de Contreras,
                                was far from
cheerful. It was received in November so perhaps things
have changed since then. You were contemplating a move
to Switzerland. If you've gone, you will never read this
letter but I write because I shall soon be on my travels
to Australia. I'm dreading it; you possibly know that
there the English are most unwelcome. I am fully ex-
pecting beer cans to be thrown on to the stage. Even
the man who has arranged this trip does not deny that
there will be hostility.
                        I have eight weeks to do and
shall be back in August for a good cry before going to
America. I shall try to live in the States forever but
may find this impossible: my age will make it unlikely
that I shall be allowed to become an immigrant but I
might gradually become a resident alien.
                                        In your letter
you were unsure of what I had meant about Mr. Bennett. He
sold "A CHORUS LINE" to the movies for five million dollars which I hoped to help him spend on a musical of my
book. This never happened. Now Mr. Elkins plans to
make a stage production of it out whether in America or
here or both and whether a musical or a straight play I
have no idea. While I am in America I shall be a sort of
sales adjunct to him so that no one forgets me before all
these decisions have been taken.
                                In the mean time I am
rushing round England to various provincial towns of which
you will never have heard. Audiences are amazingly polite;
they do not always agree with what I say but they are seldom
hostile.
        I hope that, if you have not left South America,
things have now been smoothed out for you and that the boys
have struggled through their examinations which, when you
last wrote, still hung over them.
                                Education is a complete
waste of time but what else can you do with children? Where
on earth can you put them but school?

        Love to everybody. . .

                QUENTIN CRISP

QUENTIN OUTLINES HIS RESERVATIONS ABOUT THE AUSTRALIAN TOUR

interview he was taken for lunch. As he walked through the streets of Toronto he was stared at, especially by a number of the city's 'pretty boys'. His hosts were surprised he wasn't more flattered by this. Quentin said, however, that having been a pretty boy he knew how 'self-regarding, feeble and generally not worth the money this species can be'. Not only was he embracing his new life, but he was rejecting his old one.

After Canada there were numerous other visits, amongst them a tour of Australia which ended up being a disaster. Before going Quentin told his Promoter that the Australians 'hated the English at the best of times and would take particular offence at him'. But the Promoter took no notice and Quentin was dispatched to the former colony. On his arrival at the airport he was met with a barrage of flashbulbs despite the time being only 7 a.m. As the car pulled away he was followed by a cameraman making a small documentary about his arrival.

Quentin wryly reflected that it seemed to him that 'though the Australians hate the English they love England much as many people love France but hate the French'. The net result was, he noted, 'I became an embodiment of the traditions of my native land even though I had spent a life time rebelling against them.' As a result he felt he was divested of his 'power to shock' and the tour failed, he felt, not because the Australians were outraged by him but rather because they were indifferent. He said he could cross the road in Melbourne and barely illicit a glance. On one occasion whilst standing in the doorway of a cinema attempting to hail a taxi, two young gentleman came up to him trying to work out whether they had or hadn't seen him on television the previous night. When they decided they had one of them came up and shook his hand and said, 'So you're homosexual, big deal!' Quentin said the men had not tried to demean him rather to comment on the folly of a world so concerned with such things.

Later in the tour, in Brisbane, he experienced another episode which taught him much about the difference between the English and Australians. He was in his hotel room when the phone rang and it was a young man of about 14. The boy had been ordered to write an essay for school about the documentary following Quentin's arrival in Australia and wandered if he could come and interview him. Quentin said he immediately realised he should not figure in a school essay beginning 'When I interviewed Mr Crisp in his hotel bedroom …', and the young man was invited backstage at the theatre where he questioned Quentin about his sex life 'without any embarrassment or teenage giggles'. This was an interesting lesson to Quentin. Much as he claimed all he wanted was integration he was made very aware that a large part of his fame depended on the fact that he was different and, to be like everyone else, was to rob him of his 'star status'. Indeed many were the times he would bemoan the death of the star and I think it was this, in part, which prompted him to say some of the more outrageous things he said in his later years. Far from being mere 'Uncle Tom' comments they were his way of making sure he remained 'other', retained his power to shock and to be kept in the news, something which he acknowledged his very survival depended on:

> *I live on the fact that I am famous and I've no idea why I am famous and so*
> *I have to cling onto everything in case it was the one thing for which I was famous.*
> *I keep on looking like this because that made me the way I'm famous and I*
> *go on saying the one liners because it made me famous. I'm in the smiling and*
> *nodding racket.*

The Australian tour was a financial disaster for the Promoter and Quentin returned to England.

I have always been American in my heart

I have always been American in my heart, ever since my mother took me to the movies in south Wimbledon.

When Quentin visited the University of St Andrews in 1975 it was the first time he had been out of England. Before 1977 he had never been outside the British Isles. By 1979 he had visited every part of the world where 'Crisperanto was spoken' but the place that had impressed him most had been New York which he visited briefly after his Canadian trip.

I have always been American in my heart ever since my mother took me to the movies in south Wimbledon. She took me to the cinema in a spirit of ostentatious condescension, the movies were for 'serving gals', people with any taste went to the theatre. But when I saw the pictures of New York on the screen I began to gibber and twitch. My mother said that what went on in the screen was vastly different from what happened in real life, but she was wrong because everyone who comes to New York from London and goes back says one thing: 'it's more like the movies than you'd ever dreamed'. And it is: they really do bring the dining room tables onto the pavement in the summer and they mop their necks with Kleenex and they say 'it isn't the heat it's the humidity'. When you walk through Manhattan people stop and tell you the story of their lives whilst the traffic lights change. I was standing at a bus stop on Third Avenue and a black gentleman went by and when he saw me he said 'well my, you've got it all on today'. And he was laughing and I laughed and I had got it all on. When I was swanning around the West End with all the other young boys on the game in the thirties I thought what a pity it is we never look at one another, we never smile. It could all be one long party, and in Manhattan it is one long party.

Resident Alien – The Play

Indeed he would later say that all the performances he had given elsewhere were 'merely a dress rehearsal for New York'.

His first visit there came about by a curious route. Thames Television bought seven consecutive evenings of American viewing time in order to sell their shows. Amongst the films shown was *The Naked Civil Servant*. Quentin said he could not imagine on which channel this was shown as the idea of

> *... any sponsor wishing to advertise in the breaks between the programme seemed ludicrous indeed unless the copy were to say if you don't eat up your Shredded Wheat, you'll end up like Quentin Crisp.*

Anyway the broadcast was made and following it Quentin was approached by a Mr Lindsay, a former Mayor of New York, a position Quentin would later say was 'only just south of God'. He wanted to interview Quentin for American television and was duly invited to Beaufort Street in London. Mr Lindsay was a good looking and silky smooth American who Quentin described as a 'new improved Mr Niven'. He arrived with a producer whose 'nerves were worn down to a stump by lack of sleep, an Italian cameraman and a lighting expert who longed only for glasses of Guinness'. Because of the size of the room Quentin and Mr Lindsay were forced to huddle together on the bed and address the same microphone rather as if in the windscreen shot of some car chase movie. Quentin never thought what was recorded would appear anywhere, but he was wrong. The interview was shown on *Good Morning America* the prime breakfast show with a viewership of eleven million people and shortly afterwards he was invited to America by the then 'darling of the Schubert Theatre group', Mr Bennett.

> *The moment I caught sight of it I wanted it and stretched my arms through the car window towards the skyscrapers like a child beholding a Christmas tree. Every street along which we drove brought back some long dead memory of some long dead movie seen when life was dreary and only the world of celluloid was rich and full. Every person on the sidewalks reminded me of the soldiers who invaded London during that happy time.*

When he arrived on Manhattan he was met at his hotel by Mr Bennett, who Quentin said was 'the very spirit of the place – a jumping up and down man of limitless hospitality who is wild about the entertainment industry'. He had arranged for Quentin to stay at the Algonquin in 'splendour which it would be ruinous to become accustomed, in a hotel suite large enough to house a Catholic family'. He was given a bed in which he said 'four people could have slept without ever being introduced' which prompted him to observe that in America everything 'is on wide screen'.

Quentin stayed in New York for two days and on his last evening Mr Bennett took him on a tour of his theatres before ending up having dinner at the temple of theatrical eating, Sardi's, where they sat at a table 'large enough for the board of a multinational company to have met'. It was just as well – at regular intervals they were joined by other diners. Amongst those he was introduced to was Max Von Sydow. One gentleman who came over said, 'Oh, is there to be a collaboration of some kind?' Mr Bennet said this was a secret, to which the man replied ironically, 'Then why are you in Sardi's?'

Quentin loved Sardi's, in it he observed the very embodiment of modern American culture with 'waiters darting around like traffic at rush hour on Brooklyn Bridge'. He said he thought that 'there was more waving, squeaking and embracing in this restaurant than anywhere else on earth' and he couldn't help contrasting it with the tight-lipped attitudes of English restaurateurs. Quentin would say that in the attitude of the staff he also saw a crucial difference between the British and American ways of life.

> *The English actually want their jobs to be boring so that they can strike, they want their friends to be dull so that they need not feel inferior to them. New Yorkers on the other hand strenuously resist all tendencies to reduce people and events to the lowest common factor.*

A friend had once said to him that in America 'everyone is rich and everyone is handsome'. Quentin said it was true but not the whole story, the word that needed adding was 'eager'.

They want to speak, they want to listen and they will endure quite a lot of inconvenience to prevent colour from being drained out of experience. They like people to be unusual in any way they know how. Visiting Englishmen they adopt and coo at them as though they were budgies that can nearly speak American.

Quentin had fallen head over heels in love with The Big Apple and his host had noted the fact. So much so that on the morning Quentin left he came to his hotel room and presented him with a large American flag. Quentin draped it around his shoulders and wore it all the way back to Heathrow as though it 'were my college scarf'. He said that, had he died on the way home 'I should have been extremely annoyed at the time but later, looking down from my cloud, I would have been content'. He would return at the earliest opportunity.

Alteration in their lives

People who cannot expect any alteration in their lives to be wrought by a deepening understanding of themselves must seek variety from external sources. Their chief hope seems to rest in a change of climate.

The reason for Mr Bennett's invite had been his wish to purchase the stage rights to *The Naked Civil Servant*. In the end he didn't buy them, but he passed on the idea to a Mr Elkins who did purchase an option. A year later, at his invite, Quentin once again crossed the Atlantic. Mr Elkins had once been a performer who had become an impresario because he 'didn't know how to do anything else'. Quentin said we may infer from that that 'promotion is where actors go when they die'. The play never happened and the project metamorphosed into a musical. It too floundered. However as a result of this visit Quentin embarked on the first of his American stage performances. The first performance he gave was at the smaller studio of the Long Wharf Theatre in New Haven where the plays by Eugene O'Neill had originally been performed.

New Haven is a university town but, for the most part, the colleges blend into the background of the town rather than becoming it's *raison d'être*. This gave the place a less stuffy atmosphere than that found in places such as Yale which Quentin never enjoyed playing in. The show was a success and the locals took him to their hearts taking him out during the day on tours of the area. In these tours they would often apologise for the provinciality of New Haven. Quentin said that had they not mentioned it he wouldn't have noticed, he was still dazzled he said by the 'bright lights' of the States. From New Haven he moved onto Washington before eventually reaching New York where he was booked to perform at the Players Theatre just off Washington Square.

The minute he saw the Players Theatre, Quentin felt it was the perfect place for him to perform: 'The inside looked like a kinky cinema.' The auditorium held about 200 people and was long and narrow. Here, for the first time, he had a proper Stage Manager who spent time selecting the right chair for Quentin to sit on and bought some ferns for the side of the stage. These would become trademark properties – so much so that his memorials on both sides of the Atlantic featured a similar set: an antique chair, a hat stand, a small table and, on it, a glass of whisky. They began quietly with a large number of previews to invited audiences in order that Quentin could prepare to face the sternest test of all: the New York critics. Mr Elkins had adapted the show and Americanised some of it. The result was that Quentin was struggling to actually remember this new version. However by the press night he had got his head round it. The critics loved it. Even the feared *New York Times* Critic, Ben Barnes, praised the show. Quentin said he felt their reaction was softened by the fact that he was 'a foreigner – nay an outcast and an old man and alone'. The show became a success, though not before the whole thing was almost destroyed.

Shortly after the press night Quentin was giving his performance when, about 20 minutes in, the lights began to flicker and 'loud noises began to emanate from the wings'. Then, without warning, all the lights went out. Someone in the audience suggested they go on as if nothing had happened but then all the lights in the theatre came on and the Theatre Manager walked from the back of the auditorium declaring that the building was on fire and requesting that the audience evacuate the auditorium. They did, and three fire trucks duly arrived with 'firemen in large helmets, big boots and carrying pick axes'. By the time the men got there the small fire had been extinguished and Quentin seized on the opportunity to have his picture taken with 'the uniformed saviours'. At the time the fire department had a policy of not employing 'known homosexuals', however the firemen agreed to pose for the picture which subsequently appeared in a magazine called *Where It's At* and was for Quentin one of the funniest he had ever had taken. It featured him standing amongst these icons of machismo complete with their handlebar moustaches and axes, and doubtless appealed to the anarchist in him: posing with the 'enemy'.

This was not the only unusual event to occur during his run. On another occasion a woman asked during the question-and-answer part of the show if Quentin thought Jesus had style. He said he had often been questioned about 'you know who' but had never been asked about his son before. As he always did before answering a religious question he asked the audience if anyone would mind him giving an answer to such a question as he wouldn't like to give offence. When someone shouted 'why stop now?' he realised it was safe to continue. Quentin said he thought style either 'resided in Mr Nazareth or his biographers' and then went on to quote from the New Testament: 'He that drinketh of this water shall thirst again.' Suddenly the house went cold and remote. Afterwards the Stage Manager advised him never to quote from the Bible on stage. Typically he laughed it off saying he thought the audience must have been 'shocked that anyone so wicked knew the Bible so well', however he had learnt another lesson and he knew it.

When not on stage Quentin completed endless rounds of press and television interviews. He had by now mastered the art of the sound bite and without much effort could give a response that would make the news' pages the following day. A fine example of this came at the end of 1978 when a journalist rang him up to ask what he thought would happen in 1979. Quentin simply said, 'Everything will get worse.'

It was around this time that he started to receive uncorrected proof copies of books from publishers who hoped he would say a few nice words for the dust jacket. This was another pattern that would repeat itself right up until the end of his life. Quentin always claimed never to read these books on account that books 'were for writing not reading'. However, he always obliged the publishers by saying a few nice things. He said he did this partly 'to avoid being attacked in the street by hoards of angry novelists'. Of course if he was paid to write something then he would actually read the book.

> *I do not dislike writing pieces of prose if they are short. When I come to the end of them, I may, with luck, still be able to remember what I said at the beginning but if I write a whole book, after a while I am overtaken by the fear that I have begun to state the opposite of what I said at the outset. I am then forced to read my first few*

chapters over again. I find rereading even my own deathless prose tedious in the extreme.

Quentin found writing books a necessary evil as, he often said, to him writing was not a way of life but a means of living.

After eleven weeks his run at the Players Theatre ended. Whilst the run had been a success and the show had been recorded for release by EMI, Quentin would later remind his readers that what was called a 'Broadway triumph' was only eleven weeks in a small unfashionable theatre in downtown New York. However it had fully introduced Quentin to New York and he vowed to himself on the flight back to London that the next time he came to New York he would not return. In 1980 he left England for good. He was 72 years old.

Now in the winter of my life

I ought to have crossed the Atlantic in early middle age and should now be coming home to die but 30 years ago my poverty and my general ineffectuality prevented me from attempting a journey so daring. Now in the winter of my life, I have been carried across the ocean as though on a plate. This astonishing piece of good fortune I must not waste.

When he arrived on the other side of the Atlantic things didn't exactly go to plan. 'When I arrived in America with all my worldly goods tied up in a little red handkerchief I was betrayed.' He had met a man who had promised him that he could stay with him indefinitely; Quentin had written to him advising him the day and the hour of his arrival but the man had not written back. For some strange reason Quentin assumed this meant everything was alright and consequently he arrived at the man's door to find him, not only unwilling to let Quentin stay, but even unwilling to open the door fully. He was forced to go and stay with his Manager in the splendour of his apartment on 39th Street. Here he stayed, sleeping on the sofa for six weeks until 'one of his spies' located him a room on the Lower East Side.

The room was even smaller than the one he had left in Beaufort Street. The whole place was little more than 50 square feet. Quentin was fond of telling people how it was a room 'in the last rooming house in New York'. Very quickly it began to resemble Beaufort Street as the dust and grime got hold. He was delighted.

This is an ideal spot. There are three floors. I am on the second. I share a bathroom in the hallway with my neighbours. There is a 'super', his name is 'Happy Phace'. He is a very tall, part-time drag queen who is very kind and lets me in when I forget my keys which happens quite often. He has a chihuahua which since it won the Taco Bell advertisement on television has been insufferable and barks every time

Take no notice of the back of this page; it is only part of
a rejected book. Q.C.

                                    The Church of the
                                    Beloved Disciple,
                                    348 West 14th. St
                                    NEW YORK 10014

                                    23rd. October '80

Thank you,
        dear Denise,
                    for your kind letter. I am not
really staying in a church but it is a safer resting place
for letters than my rather dubious room opposite. I have,
as you see, reached America and am hammering away at a Mrs.
Levitt who is my immigration lawyer in the hope of becoming a "resident alien." At the moment our plea is that I
will do work that no American will do. If this fails, I
shall "come here to join my relatives." Mrs G. now has a
telephone and we have spoken to each other at great length.
She is planning to visit New York in order to witness me
when I do a stint of addressing the multitude in a dim bar
on 6th. Avenue. How she will return in the middle of the
night to New Jersey I have no idea but, as you know, she
is infinitely resourceful and will doubtless have a distant
relative in New York whom she can nag into allowing her to
sleep on his bathroom floor.
                            At the moment I am staying in
a penthouse that belongs to a kind friend. The hospitality
of Americans is infinite. Taxi drivers are willing to take
you round the city free of charge: bus drivers shake you by
the hand; pedestrians say, "Welcome to The United States!"
                        If you possibly can, you should
come here though I am aware of your difficulties. Everyone
is rich and everyone is handsome so you could marry almost
anybody within a week.
                        I was delighted to hear from you
and sorry that most of your correspondence is with my agent.
I send you my best wishes for your health and happiness.
This message also goes for your mother and your children.
If I am granted residency here, I will write again; if not,
the whole world will know. . .

                    QUENTIN CRISP

QUENTIN ARRIVES IN NEW YORK

I go onto the landing. Oh, and there is a gentleman above who insists on putting dead mice under my door as a token of his esteem. He stopped for a while when the young lady below acquired a cat and he ran out of ammunition, unfortunately she has moved on. I am living under 'mouse arrest'.

Resident Alien – The Play

Many of the people who came to visit Quentin in those early days, and who had never been to his Beaufort Street flat but had only heard him speak of his hatred of housework, were amazed to find that he did actually live the way he professed to live. The juxtaposition of this dandyish figure telling people about the essence of style whilst living in abject squalor baffled many. Quentin explained it simply:

My mode of living only represents poverty to Americans – not to me. I live in exactly the same way I lived in London in a room which has not been dusted for 18 years. After the first four years it doesn't get any worse, It's just a question of not losing your nerve. You will be surprised how the dust accumulates. It does not lay on the surfaces you use most. It does not lie in the path between the door and the fire or the door and the stove, it's like snow, it drifts into the corners of the room.

Resident Alien – The Play

To Quentin there was a financial logic to it and to his refusal to retire.

As I say, I have to go on working because in America there will be no-one to pick me up off the streets or pay my pension. It is the way of the country. I have found there is a strange relationship between the system of a country and its people. In England the people are hostile to a man but the system is benevolent. The very old, the very young and the ill-equipped to live will always be looked after. In America everyone is friendly – almost doggie like but the system is ruthless. Once you can be pronounced unproductive, you've had it. You will end up living in a cardboard box at the corner of a street where once you occupied a mansion. That is the reason why I live in this one room in the last rooming house in New York.

It wasn't only the state of the room that amazed visitors but its location. In those days the Lower East Side was a world removed from its present status as a firmly up-coming artistic area of Manhattan. It was inhabited by drug pushers and winos and Quentin's house was almost directly opposite a chapter of the Hell's Angels. People would worriedly ask about them, concerned for his well-being and Quentin would say, 'Don't worry, they have a bad reputation but they've never murdered me.'

He was happy; on the streets of the Lower East Side he found a warmth and a generosity of spirit he had not experienced in Britain since wartime. There were so many different nationalities, races, sexes and income groups that he said he felt 'freaks like him passed unnoticed'. He often recalled a conversation he'd had with a man on a bus on Second Avenue who'd told him, 'It was the place to be if you're of a different stripe.' He said he thought that many people had wrongly assumed that all he wanted to do was provoke hostile attention when in truth what he really wanted was to be accepted, but on his terms, without having to compromise his look or his attitude. If he compromised he said, then 'all the hospitality he received would really have been meant for someone else'. In New York, as an Englishman abroad, it was meant for him.

> *[One day] I was standing at a bus stop on Third Avenue and a black gentleman went by and when he saw me he said 'well my, you've got it all on today'. And he was laughing and I laughed and I had got it all on.*

Resident Alien – The Play

In London he said someone would have been pressing their face close to his and asking the question, 'Who do you think you are?' Perhaps, more importantly, the thing he most liked about America was the fact that it was a young country with a relatively short history. Like him, it had the capacity for self-invention and the notion that the man in the street could rise to become President (however unreal in reality) was a breath of fresh air after the class ridden and divided Britain of the seventies. Also crucially, I think, it offered him a grand new audience. He needed this. Many people would say to meet Quentin Crisp once was to know him and this was true: on the second meeting you may get stories you'd heard in the first. As he said himself, 'Whilst I like my friends I am mad about strangers.' They didn't know the stories and couldn't anticipate the punch lines. America was full of strangers.

With his base firmly established he set about launching himself into his new life.

England was terrible

People ask me what I miss about England and I rack my brains such as they are and I answer my gas fire, and people say 'oh, you must miss something other than your gas fire' but I don't. England was terrible.

By the time Quentin had settled into his new life in America he was in his mid-70s and the 'product' that he had sought to develop throughout his entire life was at the peak of its powers and popularity. People knew who he was and what he stood for, the words 'Quentin Crisp' had become synonymous with a certain kind of English eccentricity and with homosexuality.

Perhaps more importantly he knew exactly who he was, he had always believed far more strongly in nurture than nature and through careful self-nurturing he had overcome handicaps which would, and did, destroy many others. The net result was he was now a successful writer – *The Naked Civil Servant* had sat in the bestseller lists – and an international celebrity. The TV adaptation had been hugely successful and influential and had been seen throughout the world; his one-man show, an area in which he had previously failed, had run on both sides of the Atlantic to critical acclaim; and his follow-up book telling the story of his journey to America *How to Become a Virgin* had also enjoyed a widespread readership. He now was a permanent resident in the city of his dreams and regularly invited to what he called the 'peanut and champagne circuit' and a panelist on numerous television shows. He had truly entered 'the profession of being'.

To many pensioners this would have been a cue to slow up and ease themselves into retirement; but in many ways Quentin was living his life in reverse. Having waited until his mid-60s to gain any widespread recognition for his talents he was not about to retire from the fray now.

Every day through the mail I receive invites to Broadway theatre first nights, to secret screenings of unpopular films, to the opening of galleries exhibiting works by obscure artists and to parties for someone no-one has ever heard of in dim basements. I can't go to all of them but I must go to some or they will cease to send them and I shall be cut off from the world. These events serve a dual purpose – they keep me in touch with the press and, if I can live on peanuts and champagne, I need never buy food again. I have learned not to flinch at the flashes from the cameras and to nod when I have not heard what is being said, which is increasingly often as I am going deaf. I never refuse to be photographed. That is no easy thing as every fifth person in Manhattan is a professional photographer and I never refuse to answer questions however trivial they may be. I cannot endow the wing of a hospital or university. I do not have the money, all I can give to repay America is my infinite availability.

This concept, that these appearances were a way of repaying America, was something he would repeat often. Perhaps it was true, but there was also the less generous truth which he himself owned up to in *The Naked Civil Servant*, that he was an incorrigible show-off. Quentin was never happier than when he was being photographed or interviewed. He lived for it. These events all gave him the same opportunity: to offer himself 'gift wrapped to the world'. As a result he repeated the policy that he had had in London of not going ex-directory. He began to receive a steady stream of visitors to his East Third Street room who would take him out to lunch and receive their own one-man show.

I have had a week in the eye of the hurricane of promotion. I have spent a lot of time lurking in my room and in little neighbouring restaurants welcoming visitors from England. Perhaps I should buy a lamp and stand on a rock in New York harbour.

Resident Alien – The New York Diaries

These encounters invariably took place in his favourite Cooper Square Diner which was legend for the size of its portions and the plainness of its cooking. Quentin always maintained he 'didn't hold with kinky food' and it suited him just fine: 'The great thing is whatever you order it tastes the same.' What is striking when one talks to some of the people who met Quentin for lunch is how each one believed he had told them something no-one else had heard and yet how, in truth, he had told everyone more or less the same thing. His life was becoming performance art. And, as in England, he still occasionally received crank calls.

> *I received one at four o'clock in the morning last week from a totally unknown caller who wanted to know if I had ever suffered from venereal disease and whether I knew that Miss Garbo had died. I answered no to the first question and yes to the second. The stranger then said with a wistful intonation, I suppose that means we shall all die. It does. Oh, and one woman rang me at 7.30 in the morning and asked me how to prevent her lipstick from smearing. Another wanted me to tell her what to do because she had allowed her hairdresser to cut her hair short and now she had decided she didn't like it.*

Resident Alien – The New York Diaries

Having established himself firmly, and having made sure his name was on the invite list for celebrity events, he set about using that notoriety.

Famous for wearing make-up

I am a man who's famous for wearing make-up, it's hardly enough.

In the early eighties Quentin made his professional stage-acting debut playing Lady Bracknell in *The Importance of Being Earnest* with the Soho Repertory Company. It was interesting that he should agree to appear in a Wilde play given his lack of respect for how 'Saint Oscar' had lived his life but then, they were paying. He also appeared in Professor Eric Bentley's production of his own play *Lord Alfred's Lover* where he played the title role.

My inclusion in the cast is the whim of Professor Bentley who will be held entirely responsible for any disgrace that is hereby brought upon the history of the American theatre.

Bentley himself would say that what 'the American theatre gained in the process was not one great British actor but one great British personality'.

Many of Bentley's friends had questioned his judgment working with Quentin who they increasingly felt held 'all the wrong opinions'. Bentley said however that during this time together he realised that his personality was not what it had commonly been supposed to be. 'I learned that his opinions – if indeed he really held opinions – were not the important thing about him.' Bentley said he was 'the strongest man he ever met' and 'not at all what the world expects an effeminate homosexual to be'. Bentley identified a crucial part of the Crisp conundrum. Take his words in abstraction and they present one picture: hear him say them and they present a quite different image. For example, I spoke to him in the wake of the crisis in Yugoslavia, and Quentin said, 'Why is Mr Clinton sending the brave and the beautiful to Yugoslavia? Let them die, they're only Europeans!' On paper it looks shockingly brutal and inhumane but to see him say the words with a twinkle in his eye was to get a quite different version and you were left wondering whether he was satirising or endorsing such opinions. With Quentin what you saw was never what you got, despite the fact that he always claimed the opposite. He truly had the outsider's eye, and whilst he seemed to hold strong opinions about everything, he knew and implicitly acknowledged in conversation that there are no absolute answers.

In 1985, Guy Kettelhack compiled *The Wit And Wisdom of Quentin Crisp* which featured edited highlights of Quentin's show and excerpts from his previous books, as well as conversations he'd had with Kettelhack. What was striking to me when I reread this book is how similar it was to the conversations I had had with Quentin 15 years later as well as to the material in *How To Have A Life-Style*. Certainly, he added to the routine, but he never came up with an entirely new 'turn'.

There was also a collection of essays on movie stars and on the business of going to the cinema. He published *How To Go To The Movies* in 1989. In it he outlined his own personal philosophy on 'the forgetting chamber'. Now, after all the years that cinema had provided a weekly release from the pain of his everyday existence, he was able to turn that experience and those recollections into memorably idiosyncratic pieces on the films and, in particular, the people who made them. His descriptions of his favourite stars were remarkable, not least for the fact that they told you as much about Quentin as the people he was writing about. And here, as elsewhere, he was not above reusing material from his one-man show or other writings. Of Joan Crawford he said:

> *There is a special glow which surrounds people who have succeeded in synthesising their professional and personal lives. Take Joan Crawford, she appeared in any number of movies in which she rose from rags to riches. In real life she finally married Mr Pepsi-Cola and she had all the luck in the world because he died. That meant she could enter the boardroom of that vast multinational empire where presumably she said 'who told you to read the minutes' just as she had done in all her movies. I once saw her at the National Film Theatre in London. A car as long as the Thames drew up and out stepped those two now famous children. They stood*

*in the lobby looking bewildered and no wonder because after about three minutes
she came out of the same car and kissed the children as though she hadn't seen
them for months. She was radioactive with belief in herself.*

Of Judy Garland he said:

*The worship of Miss Garland has turned out to be more peculiar and less
ephemeral than this customary public interest. It started with her failure. On the
first day of shooting* Annie Get Your Gun *Miss Garland was replaced by Miss
Hutton. The world shook. It was not possible to think that the star of so many nice
movies had done anything wrong so she became a self-evident victim. From this
point onwards she attracted the homosexual vote. These men did not so much
champion her cause as wallow in her defeat. … Miss Garland's ambitions on the
screen were exceptionally modest, while in real life the world demanded such a lot
of her. I think it was the combination of these two factors that raised this unhappy
song-and-dance girl to be the patron saint of a group of men who, however much
they differ in other respects, are united in the idea that they are persecuted by a
heartless world.*

Of Greta Garbo he commented:

*A critic has said of Miss Garbo that in her pictures she always seemed to be the
only member of the cast who had read the script to the bitter end. She was the only
one who knew it would all turn out badly. One might go further and say tragedy
was her element.*

Quentin's taste in films was, not surprisingly, American and rather old school.
He loved the big romantic narratives that Hollywood did so well and disliked
British and European films with their altogether more proletarian casts,
fragmented narratives and, as he saw it, lack of grandeur. To Quentin the
cinema was a place of romance and escapism, and he mourned the passing of
the divas and the great stars he had been brought up with. At one point in the
book he says,

It is difficult for anyone who has had the misfortune to be born into this age of

*appalling equality to imagine how brightly shone the stars on younger and happier
nights.*

Even in the cinema the homogenisation of the world was something he railed
against but, as even he admitted,

> *There is no way back to Eden; we have eaten the bitter apple of equality to the
> very core, dragging the gods down to our own mean level. From now on, our lives
> will consist of a relentless, exhausting pursuit of pleasure instead of a quest for the
> holy grail of happiness. Our talk will be of money and sex, never of power or beau-
> ty.*

He also rejected the modern notion of stars being like their audience. Quentin
argued that the public cannot make a star but a star creates themself. 'A star
has to be someone we could not have invented if we had sat up all night.'

Not only were there other books but there was a considerable amount of
journalism. He contributed film reviews to, amongst others, *The New York
Times* and he began a regular diary column in the now defunct *Christopher
Street* magazine in which he told readers of his life on the 'peanut circuit'.
What's surprising is, that when one rereads them now, the number of theatre
shows Quentin went to. Despite the fact that he said he much preferred the
movies there were very few weeks when he didn't recount to his readers his
adventures in the dim world of the theatre, both off and on Broadway.

One such weekly instalment was devoted to a show featuring the performer
Bette Bourne, who a decade later would play Quentin in my play and
become, in the words of Ian Shuttleworth of the *Financial Times* newspaper,
'also one of the stately homos of England'. Quentin began,

> *I received a telephone call from Mr Bourne of Bloolips demanding that I attend
> a performance of a play called* Sarrasine *put on by an English company, Gloria.
> I am Mr Bourne's slave, so, last Thursday I went to 19th Street to the Bessie
> Schonberg Theatre (who was she?).*

He did not let slip what he thought of the show.

The *Christopher Street* diaries are very different to his early memoirs which were so much about the struggle to be himself. Now he was totally accepted, his writing became that of a 'dilettante, a butterfly on the wheel' and his observations on the people and places he went were often a delight. After one theatre visit he declared, 'It seems to me that every theatregoer throughout the world is a middle class, middle-aged woman with a broken heart.' Following an invite to visit an art gallery he intoned,

> *I rarely visit galleries, for two reasons: the first is that there is never anywhere to sit and the second is that I do not understand art. When people ask me what I've got against pictures, I can only reply 'What have you got against the wall?'*

After a visit to Richard Attenborough's film Ghandi he wrote, 'Apparently it won every possible award except the one for costume design, presumably because sheets have only to be arranged rather than tailored.' He also wrote of his own appearances in the movies,

> *Being in a film is like giving birth. For a few hours after, while the memory of the suffering is clear in your mind, you swear you will never go through such an ordeal again, but when sufficient time has elapsed and the memory has faded, you have another baby or make another film.*

The *Christopher Street* diaries were eventually compiled into a collection which produced his last major book, *Resident Alien*, published in 1995.

In the late eighties Mr Sting, as Quentin loved to call him, released a hit single *Englishman In New York.*

> *Manners maketh man as someone said*
> *He's our hero of the day*
> *Be yourself no matter what they say*
> *Be yourself no matter what they say ...*

QUENTIN ON THE FILM SET

Quentin was in the video – walking coolly down the streets of the Lower East Side, looking every inch a man at ease with himself having finally found home and arrived at who he wanted to be.

There was also other journalism for papers – such as *The Manchester Guardian* for whom he wrote an infrequent column for his friend Simon Hattenstone – a column that became even less frequent towards the end of his life when he ceased to be able to type.

My left hand is now paralysed so I can no longer get my arm in my shirt as I would like. It also prevents me from typing which restricts the amount of publications I can contribute to. I write for only one newspaper now, The Manchester Guardian, *and there a man called Hattenstone rings me once a month and asks me what I have been doing and where I have been and when I tell him he says 'I'll put you onto the copy department', and there there is a women who types so fast that she can type faster than I can speak and she gets it all down and they send a cheque.*

Resident Alien – The Play

Alongside the writing he became the subject of yet another documentary, this time a feature-length piece entitled *Resident Alien* by Jonathan Nossiter which was released in 1990. The film came about after Nossiter had worked with Quentin on the set of *Fatal Attraction* in which he had played a cameo which was later cut from the finished film. *Resident Alien* was a 90-minute portrait of Quentin, his circle of friends and his New York life. Nossiter said,

People in New York always walk round as if they are in the middle of a movie, whether they are being filmed or not. In that sense Quentin is the ultimate New Yorker. His whole physical persona has been devised in order to project himself as a film, for the entertainment of the general public. In New York it's gobbled up. My film functions as a contemporary portrait of an expatriate, but the focus is really on this man, in this city and what the two have to do with each other. For all his apparent Englishness, there's something about Quentin's ability to promote himself and turn his whole persona into a character for sale, in a completely charming way, that's peculiar to New York. He is a kind of King of the Bohemians here.

The film cut shots of Quentin's life amongst the poets, playwrights and painters of the Lower East Side with fictional scenes like the surreal black and white encounter with his 'representative on earth' John Hurt. At one point Quentin talks about Hurt and delivers a memorable bon mot: 'Mr Hurt is born to play victims. He played me and then he played Caligula, which is only me in a sheet.'

When the film was first shown to preview audiences, Quentin was called on to do a lot of promotional work, often involving long journeys across the country. By the time the film opened to the press he confessed to being exhausted by it all.

> *The worst is over. At least I think it is. For a while the journeys became ever more circuitous; the limousines longer, the interviews more repetitive and the parties even noisier. ... Now the film is on its own. I am inevitably blasé about its chances of making money or bringing anybody fame. Because of my great age my future is now – if it hasn't already passed.*

It received mixed reviews. Some of the critics said Quentin had come across as 'opaque', to which Quentin took great exception.

> *As far as I know I have never given an evasive reply to any question about my ideas or events in my life. My responses are aphoristic, not in order to conceal my meaning but because they have been made so often they have become crystallised if not fossilised.*

The film was compared unfavourably with *The Naked Civil Servant* and some said it told the viewer nothing new about Quentin. Quentin said, 'How could it? *The Naked Civil Servant* was made when I was already 66 – long past the age when I could be overtaken by any major change other than decay.' That said, the film enjoyed some success and was shown on television and played in a number of festivals and cinemas throughout America and beyond.

In the nineties, when in his mid-80s he amazingly developed a film career. I say 'developed' because back in the sixties and seventies he made at least two film appearances in Ann Wolf's *Captain Busby*, a 15-minute black and white film by Philip O'Connor, and as the King in *Hamlet* alongside a youthful Helen Mirren. His appearances at the end of his life were on much bigger budgets though.

In 1993, at the age of 85, he appeared as an over-rouged and voluptuously becurled Queen Elizabeth I in Sally Potter's film of Virginia Woolf's *Orlando*, and in 1994 he has a cameo part in Jonathan Demme's *Philadelphia* alongside Tom Hanks and Morgan Freeman. In 1995 he played a lab assistant in Sting's film *The Bride*. He also wasn't above doing the odd advertisement, such as the one for Impulse perfume which in a way showed how far things had come since *The Naked Civil Servant* was written featuring as it did a gay couple at its heart. He also appeared in ads for Nike trainers – he had assumed the status of an icon.

In 1996, he performed the *Alternative Queen's Speech* for Channel 4 from the Plaza Hotel and from a carriage riding regally around Central Park. Predictably certain members of the moral majority were outraged that it should be shown at exactly the same time as the other Queen was on BBC 1 addressing the nation from Balmoral. The broadcast wasn't vintage Crisp and at times he seemed curiously stilted, as if reading from an autocue that he didn't want to read from. That said, it contained a quota of amusing material and he couldn't help berating the English for being hideous and telling the viewers how much better life was in America. I don't think the broadcast did anything to endear him to the British public or press but, as ever, it kept him in the news.

There was also an extremely unlikely appearance on David Frost's *Through the Keyhole*, the television show in which a celebrity panel are asked to name the occupant of the house they see footage of. Not surprisingly the panel quickly identified the flat as Quentin's; another example of how famous Quentin had become by simply being as much like himself as possible.

46 East 3rd. Street,
NEW YORK   10003
212:254:0508

12th. December '95

Thank you,
            dear Mr. and Mrs. Ramsay,
                               for your kind
letter. What a wild time you do have -- whizzing
off to France all the time!
                         I remain fixed here but
am quite content with my fate. A letter appeared
in a Philadelphia paper asking why I was living 'on
Welfare! I'm not but it is worrying because, if Mr.
Clinton hears of this, he will deport me.
                                   Actually,
I DO receive 'social security' cheques for huge amounts
like 1,000 dollars each month though I have never worked since I came here. I've gone into the smiling and
nodding racket in a big way. It beats work any day.
I'm in a lot of 'shoe-string movies' made in dim
cellars on The Lower East Side of Manhattan. They
never see the light of day or the dark of a cinema
but are sold straight to videostores. Its all very
strange but I ask no questions.
                        I'd quite forgotten
about the Payne family. What a strange lotvthey were!
I used to go and stay with them when I was young and
starving. They wre very kind to me. So now they are
all gone.

        Your patriarch.

        QUENTIN CRISP
                       I have quite lost all
sensation in the fingers of my left hand(A stroke?
Diabetes? What ?). It makes typing very difficult.

QUENTIN'S 'SHOE-STRING MOVIE' APPEARANCES, WITH SAD POST SCRIPT NOTE

Alongside his television appearances he continued to perform his one-man show and go and talk 'wherever his fare was paid'. He signed up with a promoter called Charles Lago, an ex-policeman who Quentin never tired of saying he had 'become enslaved to'. Lago toured him around America giving talks. For a man approaching 90 it was a punishing schedule and one that his friend, Penny Arcade, later told me she didn't think he was up to. He also made a series of appearances with Arcade herself at an off-Broadway theatre called Performance Space 122 in the East Village, a venue Quentin loved to call 'the ruined school'. In these appearances, Arcade interviewed Quentin in front of an audience and attempted to get below Quentin's glittering surface. He was not impressed by this:

> *Very graciously it transpired that what Miss Arcade longs to unearth in the course of this series of two-hour sessions is some hitherto hidden aspect of my nature. She obviously doesn't believe that my one desire in life is to please the public. She thinks – nay, hopes – that underneath my sickeningly ingratiating image there is another angry self, waiting to burst forth. I am infinitely willing to cooperate in this voyage of discovery but I fear there is no hidden treasure at the end of it. What little you see is all you are likely to get.*

Resident Alien – The New York Diaries

There are very few people who believe that they ever did see another Quentin Crisp from the one he intended his audience to see. However, the Executor of his will, Phillip Ward, who spent a lot of time with Quentin shortly before his death, argues that in his last days a different, much less composed and altogether more angry Quentin would emerge. Ward told me that much of that anger was about the way he had been treated in his youth in England. It was, he said, as if Denis Pratt re-emerged.

Alongside these public appearances, Quentin continued to be interviewed ceaselessly by a press hungry for the kind of controversial copy he could be relied upon to supply.

> *You see when I lived in England my old age was taken care of by Mrs Snatcher.*

When the day came when I could no longer see or hear or walk she would spread her iron wings over me. Mrs Thatcher ascended the throne during one of my early exploratory visits to America. At that time hardly an evening passed without someone asking me my opinion of England's Prime Minister. I thought and still think she was a star and I repeatedly said so. I once gave a talk and said as much and afterwards a young woman tackled me in the street and said 'I hope you realise you gave all the wrong answers'. When my humble apologies finally subsided, she added 'you are supposed to be against Mrs Thatcher'. I was obviously expected to take politics seriously – I never have. Of course if I had been born in China, Russia or Cuba I would have been shot. Then as I stood before the line of rifles I would have said 'hold your fire, I want to vote'. In Britain going to the polls is a waste of time. There are really only two factions: the Tories and the Labourites and whichever is in power it doesn't take long for people to start moaning 'what went wrong with the Labour (or Conservative) party?' It came to power: that's what went wrong. The question is as pointless as asking 'what went wrong with our marriage?' We got married; that's what went wrong. Politics are not an instrument for effecting social change they are the art of making the inevitable appear to be a matter of wise human choice. Politics are not for people, they are for politicians – a medium in which a person can suspend his monstrous ego. The only benefit that can be derived by ordinary mortals from any of these vocations is that they provide us with someone on whom we can focus our attention – even our passions – at least in a manner less fatuous than soccer. It is this human need that Mr Disraeli, Mr Lloyd George, Mr Churchill and Mrs Thatcher fulfilled so well. It was amazing, she ruled the world and she was a woman. It's just a shame she couldn't have stayed a woman.

Resident Alien – The Play

His comments about Mrs Thatcher were made when he first arrived in New York but he continued to repeat them right up until the end of his life. Similarly he continued to air his views on the 'gay community' long after many in it had ceased to wear the fashions he spoke of.

The gay community, because it insists on being equal with real people, has decided that homosexual men are not an inferior race and so parade an egregious masculine image, wearing crew-cut hair, a kitchen tablecloth shirt, pre-ruined jeans, tractor boots and a small moustache if not a full beard. They mate with other gargoyles of masculinity, scorning or regarding with pitying contempt those of us who cannot rise to such manliness. There is now no normal or quasi-normal masculine-feminine, satyr-nymph, pursuer-pursued courtship in the gay world and come to think of it in the real one either where woman have decided to be people.

And one of his most famously controversial comments came following the death of Diana, Princess of Wales, in a Paris car crash.

Well I did lose the love of all the homosexual men in America in a single night because I said that I thought Princess Diana was trash and got what she deserved. She was Lady Diana before she was Princess Diana so she knew the racket. She knew that royal marriages have nothing to do with love. You marry a man and you stand beside him on public occasions and you go like this and for that you never have a financial worry until the day you die. And everywhere you go you are photographed. What more does a woman want? You see English kings have always behaved badly William IV had ten illegitimate children; Queen Adelaide would never have divorced him. Edward VII behaved so outrageously with his little friends that the English public knew their names – Lillie Langtry, Mrs Cornwallis West, Rosa Lewis – but Queen Alexandra would never have divorced him; and when he lay dying she said 'let Mrs Keppel be sent for'. Now isn't that wonderful, she was just as beautiful as Princess Diana and she was the Queen of England and she was his wife and she knew she didn't matter. What gave Diana the idea that she mattered? My agent went mad, my editor says you are so nice to people and then you go and say this. But they don't understand, I don't say things to be liked, I say them because I mean them.

Resident Alien – The Play

Even though he would always tell his audiences, 'I only wish to say the words you want to hear', he couldn't resist speaking his mind. The solution he hit upon was to tell them what he wanted them to hear but in the way they wanted to hear it. The wit was the fluid in which he suspended his most controversial thoughts. It often seemed that, within Quentin, there were two

QUENTIN DOING LUNCH

profound needs at play: the need to be liked; and the need for exactly the opposite. Penny Arcade described him to me as 'masochistic' and others think he suffered from a kind of internalised homophobia and there is no doubt that at times the right-wing press latched onto his comments for their own homophobic agendas. Even after his death the *Daily Mail* published a full page piece with a huge by-line quote from Quentin that read, 'Homosexuality is a curse and I wouldn't wish it on anyone.'

Despite the fact that he spent so much time in press interviews denouncing England and saying how glad he was to have escaped old Blighty, he still made a number of visits back there (more than he ever really advertised). When he visited London he would stay at the Chelsea Arts Club where he was a member. His penultimate visit came in the late nineties when he was invited to a screening of *The Naked Civil Servant* at The Everyman Cinema in Hampstead. Here he was able to meet up with some of his oldest friends including the Director of the film, Jack Gold. It was during this penultimate trip that he was able to return to Old Compton Street and the streets of his youth.

Old Compton Street was very strange the only thing that was untouched was the pubs. They were in the same position, decorated in the same way, with the same people standing in the same positions, drinking the same drinks. Everything else was altered, there were chairs and tables, and there were people sitting at the chairs and tables and talking and laughing and waving. Quite un-English I was unnerved by it. I'd never seen anything like it in the whole of my life.

Interview with Quentin Crisp, 1999

However, despite clearly being a little impressed with the changes wrought in his favourite streets, he couldn't resist a dig.

The English are an island people and they haven't accepted foreign ideas since that unpleasant business with the Normans but now they've become Americanised and eventually the whole world will become Americanised and won't that be wonderful.

Interview with Quentin Crisp, 1999

By 1998 his health was fading. He was suffering from eczema, a paralysed hand and an enlarged heart. He spent some time in hospital, though the circumstances remain vague, and in typical style he mythologised the whole episode.

I went to hospital through no fault of my own. I was sitting innocently in my room and the door bell went and three policemen burst into the hall so I ran into this room and tried to remove all signs of sin from this room and then an ambulance came and I said I ordered no ambulance and all the policeman said 'what' and so I went downstairs again and opened the door and there were half the occupants of the block, my landlord and a man called Sorrentino who I had said I would see on that day and I extended a heavily bejewelled hand in perfunctory greeting and one of the policeman said very forcefully in my ear 'get into the van it's snowing' so I got into the van with Mr Sorrentino and one of the policeman and was whisked away to a hospital where my arrival was treated as though it had been long awaited but was by no means welcome and I was put on a stretcher and was whisked down corridors into an elevator where the occupants looked down onto me coldly and I was whisked up to the twelfth floor and emptied out onto a bed like rubbish being emptied out of a wheelbarrow and after five days I thought this is ridiculous so I got up and I dressed and a nurse said where are you going and I said home and she said you can't go without a doctor's permission so I went out onto the landing and said to a man who went by 'are you a doctor?' and he said 'yes' and I said 'can I go home?' and he said 'yes' and I went home and when I told this story to somebody they said 'you sure do go with the flow' and I never found out why I was in hospital.

Interview with Quentin Crisp, 1999

He told interviewer after interviewer that he was ready for the end.

I'm ready for death but I just won't die. I once sat opposite a little old lady in a train carriage near Bromley and overheard her say to someone '… and then after 25 years, my husband died'. I was just about to look gravely at the floor when she added 'and oh, the relief'. I understand her utterly.

Resident Alien – The Play

However, he continued to keep up a punishing schedule of appearances for Charles Lago at Authors on Tour. In late 1998, the end of his 89th year, in the depths of a freezing cold New York winter he embarked once again on a performance off-Broadway of his one-man show, *An Evening with Quentin Crisp,* in a theatre 'without heating'. The show played over Christmas and his 90th birthday. It began a chain of events which would see my late arrival in the story and lead ultimately to his death in, of all places, his hated England.

QUENTIN PREPARING FOR HIS ONE-MAN SHOW

I want to die a significant death

I want to die a significant death, I don't want a lot of people stood round an iron bedstead saying 'I thought he'd died years ago'.

The show opened on Quentin's 90th birthday and was amazingly – given his age and physical condition – judged a success. So much so that English producers, Paul Spyker and Guy Chapman, flew into New York especially to see it and to try to persuade Quentin to come back to England one more time. They were unsuccessful. Quentin later said to me he just couldn't face returning to the country of his birth again and anyway didn't think his health was up to it.

In the summer of that year, with Quentin's health deteriorating further, I went to France to write the play *Resident Alien*. I decided the first half of the show would feature Quentin preparing to meet a Mr Brown and Mr Black from England who were going to put his thoughts on 'how to be happy' on the internet 'for the whole world to enjoy' and the second half would be him dealing with the fact that they had stood him up and so having to prepare his own fried egg lunch before eventually receiving a phone call from somebody else who wants to take him out the following day. It meant that the action of the play could test out Quentin's assertion that what mattered was 'not what other people thought of you but what you thought of yourself'. Under pressure, having been 'stood up', could he hold his nerve? It also meant that having not been able to give his performance to his visitors he had a good reason to give it to the audience in Act Two.

I returned to England at the end of June and with Bette Bourne and Mike Bradwell we began work, editing and chopping and changing the piece. The date for the opening night was set at 10 November. The Designer of the play, Geoff Rose, still needed more pictures of Quentin's room for the design and

BETTE BOURNE AS QUENTIN IN THE PLAY RESIDENT ALIEN

when I learnt that Alex Gammie, the Bush Theatre's Press and Publicity Officer was going on holiday to New York, we asked her to visit Quentin and get the photos and video footage. I rang Quentin and asked if it would be alright for Alex to come and see him and take some photographs. Quentin agreed and we set a time and date.

Unfortunately when Alex arrived Quentin had clearly forgotten she was coming and he greeted her without his trademark outfit. The sight of her with photographers did not please him. However, he reluctantly let her in and took her to his room quickly donning his 'uniform'. He then allowed the photographers in. It wasn't until 20 minutes into the conversation that he finally realised who she was and why she was there. 'Oh, this is for the play,' he said; and Alex duly got the photographs she needed and left.

Though I didn't know this at the time the fact that he had forgotten she was coming along with the fact that she had brought not one but two photographers, had really annoyed him. He told Phillip Ward later that he felt intruded upon by the photographers taking pictures of everything in his flat, including he said 'the contents of his wastepaper basket'. His annoyance did not go away.

In October 1999, the Bush sent out press releases for the play. The *Daily Telegraph* diary, Peterborough, got hold of one and phoned Quentin to ask what he thought of the show. Quentin exacted his revenge. He said he was 'dreading the play' fearing we were going to 'send him up'. Previously when he had seen Bette Bourne perform he had seen him in vaudevillian 'Bloolips' shows – he had no idea he was a classically trained actor before he got into 'radical drag' and this, combined with the unfortunate visit of the photographers, had convinced him that we were somehow in the business of mocking him. Penny Arcade recalls Quentin's concerns and remembers telling him that 'Bette was a serious person'. But he was not convinced and it is revealing that, despite his assertion that he simply 'went with the flow', he did not like the idea of his image being destroyed, and why would he? This image was his life's work.

BETTE BOURNE ON STAGE IN THE PLAY RESIDENT ALIEN

Mike Bradwell and myself were furious that, having agreed to the project and having allowed us to invest considerable time and money, he now seemed to be trying to undermine it. We were also baffled (at this stage we had no idea about his fury toward the photographers). I immediately wrote a response which the *Daily Telegraph* published the day after saying that I was surprised by the fact that Quentin wasn't happy about the show given that he had signed a contract agreeing to it.

In mid-October I heard a rumour that Quentin was planning a two-week national tour of his own one-man show with his London performances coinciding with our's. Naturally, I was not pleased. When we had conceived the show it was with the solid expectation that Quentin would never return. Now not only was he coming, but he was coming at exactly the same time. However it was his prerogative. I phoned him to check the facts and he confirmed he was coming in November and I wished him well and we agreed to do some publicity for both projects together.

In late October, with rehearsals for the play under way, we heard rumours that Quentin was not well. Bette phoned him. He told Bette he had a 'hernia as big as an orange' and people were telling him not to come. I spoke to him and he said his friends were advising him not to make the trip. But then, suddenly, with even his English Producer Mark Ball saying they 'felt strongly' he would cancel, he changed his mind and confirmed the tour.

A few days later a journalist from the *The London Evening Standard* called me and said he was going to interview Quentin about the play. Alarmed at the prospect, I phoned Quentin, 'You will say nice things won't you?' To which he impishly replied, 'I'll try.' He was true to his word and lavished praise on the project.

The play opened at the Bush Theatre on 10 November 1999 and thankfully received excellent notices. The *Financial Times* said Bourne was 'one of the most compelling performers he had ever seen on a stage' and that he 'as much as Crisp was now one of the stately homos of England'. Benedict Nightingale writing in *The Times* said, 'Bourne is superb, funny, touching, sometimes even profound.' *Time Out* said the play 'did for Quentin Crisp what *Jeffrey Bernard is Unwell* did for Jeff and turned a solitary man into a singular entertainment'. And, *The London Evening Standard* said, after praising the show and Geoff Rose's 'fantastically grubby set', that it was now eagerly anticipating Quentin's arrival to 'compare and contrast as they say'.

A way of ending it

You must have a way of ending it on your own terms. And the easiest way is to commit suicide. Suicide is the style in death otherwise you will be left on an iron bed in a rented room with people standing round saying he can't last much longer. But I don't commit suicide, and I know I should because I'm occupying space on television that could be occupied by younger people but I'm a sissy.

Meantime, in New York, Quentin was doing publicity for his own tour and an article appeared in the *Daily Express* in which he again told the readers that he wasn't happy about the play 'not happy at all'. By now we had rediscovered our sense of humour about Quentin's pronouncements and we subscribed to the adage that all publicity was good publicity (much easier now that the play was selling tickets).

Early on the morning of Sunday 18 November, Quentin's plane touched down at Manchester airport. It was a typical Mancunian day: misty and grey. Quentin was pushed through customs in a wheelchair by his travelling companion 'Chip', Charles Snell of Authors on Tour. The pair were met on the other side by the English Promoter of the tour, Mark Ball. Mark escorted them to his car and set off to drive them to the Victorian terrace house of Emma Ferguson in Chorltum-cum-Hardy a suburb of south Manchester. Quentin had had a great time on the flight and was 'genuinely surprised', said Mark, that he had been recognised as much as he had and had been treated so splendidly by the British Airways' staff who had given him a constant supply of food and drink. On the way into Manchester, despite his tiredness, Mark said Quentin launched into his familiar anecdotes, even after almost twelve hours of travelling he could not stop performing. Unfortunately, Mark got lost on the way to Emma's house and after a long period of driving around the area finally phoned her. She agreed to come and meet them in the centre of town. She did this, and the party then followed her eventually arriving at her house at 11 a.m. Emma had lit a fire and prepared tea and crumpets and cake. Not surprisingly she said, 'Quentin was very tired.'

Whilst she served the refreshments, Quentin sat on the sofa and chatted to her young son, Keir, about spiders. Mark remembers Quentin telling Keir in detail about the difference between tarantulas and scorpions. Emma showed him *The Guardian Guide* which featured coverage about his tour, but she said he didn't seem overly interested. He said he would like to sleep. Emma asked him if he wanted to go upstairs, he said 'No', as the steps were steep and he could barely walk. Emma brought him a quilt from upstairs and he went to sleep on the sofa. At around 1 p.m. she had to go out. Two hours later she returned to find Quentin alone and distressed. She said he had 'had an accident' after being unable to climb the stairs unaided to go to the lavatory. She told him not to worry and sorted everything out. Chip later returned and she offered them both more tea and brandy. Emma said she was surprised that Quentin 'didn't seem to know where he was going' on the tour and couldn't for the life of her, given his physical frailty, 'see how he was going to be able to perform his show'. Mark, however, felt that, though physically frail, he was more than up to the task.

By 7 p.m. Quentin was falling asleep on the sofa and said that he wanted to go to bed. She asked him if he wanted to eat. He said, 'No.' Between her and Chip they managed to get him up the stairs, 'on his bottom, one step at a time'. On the landing she showed him into his room. He said, 'Good night.' It was the last time she saw him alive.

That night her son was restless and she was woken by him on a couple of occasions, she says in retrospect he 'seemed to sense something was wrong'. At 3 a.m. she thinks she heard Quentin get up and use the lavatory. The next morning at 8 a.m. there was still no sign of him at breakfast. Concerned she asked Chip if she should go and wake him. According to Emma, Chip said it was better to let him sleep in. At 8.30 a.m., getting slightly anxious that she had heard no noise, she went up to his room. She could get no response when she knocked on the door. Worried, she went in.

Quentin was on the bed. His hair was in his face, in his hand was a bottle containing his angina pills and, all around, the sheets were scattered with the remainder of the tablets. Alongside the bed, though out of view and not discovered by Emma for another three days, was the brandy bottle from which she had poured him his last drink the previous evening. It had been half full but was now empty, and to this day she has no idea how it got up the stairs and into Quentin's room given that he could not climb the stairs himself. On his bedside table there was an empty glass and two nickels.

She tried to find a pulse but said she knew 'more or less straight away' that he was dead. She gently brushed the hair out of his face before going to call the police. Chip went downstairs and phoned Mark Ball, who was now back in Birmingham. Mark remembers him saying, 'We can't raise Quentin, I think it's serious.' A policeman arrived within minutes, neither Emma nor Chip could believe his name – it was PC Sissey. Unfortunately, when PC Sissey put out a request for assistance it must have gone out on the police airwaves because when the undertakers arrived at 11 a.m. they both knew exactly who it was they were collecting and, soon, so would the world's press.

When Mark arrived at Manchester's Piccadilly train station, Chip met him. Mark asked where Quentin was: Chip said, 'On the mortician's slab.' The two arrived back at Emma Ferguson's at noon. By now the phone was ringing and the press were outside. The three drew the curtains and hammered out a statement on Emma's old typewriter. By 1 p.m. it was headline news on BBC radio and television, and being flashed around the globe on the wires: Quentin Crisp was dead.

I had decided to have a day away from work and was travelling on the newly opened Jubilee Line extension to north Greenwich. The train was just pulling into the station when my mobile went. My friend Joan was ringing to ask if I'd heard the news: I couldn't believe it. Within minutes the phone went again, it was a journalist from the *Daily Mail* asking if I would write a tribute to him. From that point on the phone rang incessantly. I jumped in a taxi – by the time I got back to my home in Ladbroke Grove a photographer was on my doorstep and the answer machine was overloaded with messages from the press. I spent the next two hours trying to write a tribute for the next day's deadline. At 7.30 p.m. I finally faxed it off and, dumbstruck, went round to Bette Bourne's house in Colville Terrace. There was Bette, his partner Paul Shaw, my then partner Nathan Evans, and Bette's friend, Stuart Feather. We decided there should be no mourning and we cracked champagne and spent the night remembering Quentin. It was a hugely celebratory evening and at one point Stuart proposed a toast to Quentin and to Bette. 'The queen is dead, long live the queen.' It wasn't until the next morning, looking over the papers with a hangover, that it all really sank in, and I realised that he really had gone. Despite what he had said, he had seemed indestructible.

The next day the press coverage was massive, both in Britain and the States. His death was front-page news in *The Guardian, The Independent, The Times* and the *Daily Telegraph* and given substantial coverage in all the tabloids. *The Independent* said 'Stateliest Homo In England Dies at 90' before devoting an entire inside page and a large obituary to him. The *Daily Telegraph* said 'Quentin Crisp, 90 dies back home in England' and it too featured a full page obituary. *The Times* had extensive coverage and a large obituary. The *Daily Express* said, 'Farewell Mr Crisp, thanks for the gaiety.' The *Daily Mail* devoted two inside pages to my tribute and to its own article. In the States, CNN ran the story for the whole of the next day and in the shops and bars of the East Village candles were lit and pictures of Quentin placed in windows. According to one New Yorker 'the Lower East Side had lost its Mother Teresa'.

By this stage, Bette was very upset and we didn't know whether he would go on and perform the play that night. In the end he decided to go ahead and a full house sat through the most strange experience. What just 48 hours earlier had been a celebration suddenly became a requiem. Quentin was alive, but only through his words and as *The Sunday Times* Critic, Robert Hewison, who was in the audience that night said, 'When the play opened a virtual Crisp could joke about his prospects for his virtual obituary, now that Crisp has died he lives on only in Bourne's artful reproduction.' After he spoke the last line – 'To life, a funny thing that happens to you on the way to the grave' – Bette silenced the audience and made the simplest of speeches. It began, 'As you all know yesterday we lost Quentin'; and it ended with a comment made by his partner, Paul Shaw, 'His life was a triumph.' He then invited the audience to raise their glasses and toast Quentin. One hundred and thirty people, in a tiny studio theatre 'in a dim and distant district of London', as Quentin called it, raising their glasses. Truly memorable.

Meantime, back in Manchester, Chip and Mark had to go to the registry office in Manchester and register Quentin's death. The registrar, an Eric Cantona fanatic by all accounts, filled in the necessary sections for them. She had one question: 'What was his occupation?' Without hesitation Chip said, 'Being.'

Quentin's funeral was held on Wednesday 24 November at the huge, faceless Southern Cemetery in south Manchester. It was kept a secret from the press and attended only by his niece Frances Ramsay and her husband Peter, their son Tim, Chip Snell, Emma Ferguson, Mark Ball, and Chloe Poems and Divine David from the Green Room in Manchester where Quentin had been due to perform. Outside, to keep the press off the trail, the noticeboard said the cremation of 'Bernard Jones' was taking place, on the coffin there were two names, on the top Quentin Crisp, on the side Denis Pratt. Frances said a few words as did Chip, but there were no hymns and no religious element. It was over in 15 minutes and the party walked out into the cold Manchester morning. Quentin Crisp had firmly slipped into legend as he wished, 'with no fuss and no ceremony'. He hadn't quite been put out in a black bag with the rubbish as he'd requested but he had ended his time on earth in a faceless crematorium in a suburb of Manchester. His ashes were boxed up and taken away by Chip Snell for the journey back to New York. Emma Ferguson said, as she left the crematorium, she couldn't help wondering 'if it could have been prevented'. She wasn't alone.

At the time of his death Patrick Newley, Quentin's Press Agent in the eighties, was quoted as saying,

> *I am very sorry indeed to hear of his death and sadly shocked because when I spoke to him roughly two or three weeks ago in New York he was clearly not happy*

about coming over for the tour. At his age it was too much. I rather think he might still be alive if he had not come across here.

Bernard Kops, the playwright – and another man who had known Quentin for many years – said it was tragic that Quentin, who he said had applied for US citizenship, had died in Manchester. But the tour's Publicist, Ryan Levitt, said Quentin had been genuinely keen to go ahead with the tour.

It was Quentin's choice to visit Britain one last time. We gave him opportunity to cancel four weeks ago and felt strongly that he would but he said he wanted to tour England one last time.

However his old friend, Penny Arcade, recalls walking down Second Avenue just three weeks earlier and seeing Quentin burst into tears telling her he 'didn't want to go'. She controversially believes that he was pursuaded to travel against his wishes. None of this squares however with the view of Phillip Ward, the Executor of his will, or the view of his niece, Frances Ramsey. Ward believed that Quentin knew there was a strong possibility he would not return from the trip but that he wanted to go and 'perform a deliberate dance with death'. On the Thursday before he left America, Ward along with his partner and Quentin had eaten in an Indian restaurant (another revelation given that he always said he didn't hold with 'kinky food'.) Ward said Quentin was on fine form but much more reflective than his usual self. Ward said he seemed to be looking back on his life and deliberately taking stock. Frances Ramsay thinks Quentin took the gamble to come to Britain in order to die a signficant death, something he had long said he wanted. The mystery of why he came fascinated many. So why did he come?

In the immediate aftermath of his death various theories were put forward. One was that Quentin came to Britain to secure his American naturalisation. Whilst it is true that he was attempting to become American before his death and had all the neccesary papers in his possession, he did not need to return to Britain in order to achieve this. Another theory was that he was forced to come on the tour because he needed the money. This had credibility until his will was published and revealed he left $633,418 – and 62 cents. However did he really feel rich? Penny Arcade told me that when it came to money she felt 'Quentin was insane' and that he often did work when he didn't need to because, she felt, he was scared of being penniless. She believed this 'insanity' had its roots in the death of his father who, Quentin once told her, died 'because he ran out of money'. She believed Quentin never felt he had enough money. Another theory put forward was that he was forced to come by an unscrupulous promoter to whom, he often said, 'he had become enslaved'. I doubt this, and don't think his words should be taken at face value. Quentin said this about many people, it was part of his phraseology – he liked to pretend he only did as he was told but it was to some extent a pretence, after all when Guy Chapman and Paul Spyker had invited him to the UK he had turned them down. Some argue that he came to England after regretting giving the play his blessing – that he came to remind us of the real thing. The press interest in the play may have prompted him to think there was still some interest in him in the UK but surely a 90-year-old icon was not so threatened by a play in a small London theatre? Far more likely to me is the idea put forward by Phillip Ward and Frances Ramsey that Quentin knew he was going to die soon, wanted to die a 'significant death' and wanted to see his homeland one last time. Penny Arcade recalls speaking to him three days before he left when she said jokingly, 'I just wanted to say bon voyage in case you die in England.' And Quentin replied, 'Oh, that would be lovely, if I die in America in my sleep I'll only make page ten.' This theory carries even more weight when one considers that just six days before his departure he changed the terms of his will and altered the name of his Executor from Guy Kettelhack, the Editor of *The Wit And Wisdom of Quentin Crisp,* to Phillip Ward, the Compiler of his forthcoming final book, *Dusty Answers.* Ward himself believes that Quentin knew he would die in England and that the flight would put huge strain on his 90-year-old heart. In the days before his trip he was clearly firmly contemplating the ultimate destination and in his last letter to Frances Ramsay (*see* page 175), written just a few weeks before his departure, he makes clear the intense pain he is in and that he is ready for death. Given this, did his treatment on that ill-fated trip contribute to his demise? Emma Ferguson revealed to me that Quentin had not been booked in first class but that the airline had taken pity on him and given him a free upgrade. Neither had he been booked on a direct flight, having to change in

London, making the journey tortuously long for a 90-year old with a weak heart. She also said she thought the choice of her house with steep Victorian stairs was a mistake and said she felt the tour's Promoters should have worked out where the place was in advance instead of driving the tired 90-year old around Manchester in the mist. She couldn't believe, she said, that 'someone of that importance had been treated the way he had'. However, she didn't know that Quentin never travelled first class and always preferred to stay in the homes of real people rather than in high-class hotels, so much of it may well have been his own choice.

Which brings us to one final piece of the conundrum: the brandy bottle at the side of his bed and the scattered pills. Had Quentin deliberately speeded up his own demise? Emma Ferguson says she thinks he had had 'a fair bit to drink' on the plane and seemed a little drunk when he arrived. (He may however have been simply very tired.) However if, as she suspects, Quentin drank a further half bottle of brandy at her house this does seem surprising and somewhat out of character. Did this, combined with his tablets, contribute to his death? Not according to the post-morten which, whilst recording the fact that he died with pills all around him, put his death down to 'heart failure' and did not record excessive alcohol in his blood.

In death, as in life, Quentin Crisp remained an enigma. Claiming that, 'all you see is all there is', it appears he took with him more secrets to the grave than anyone could imagine.

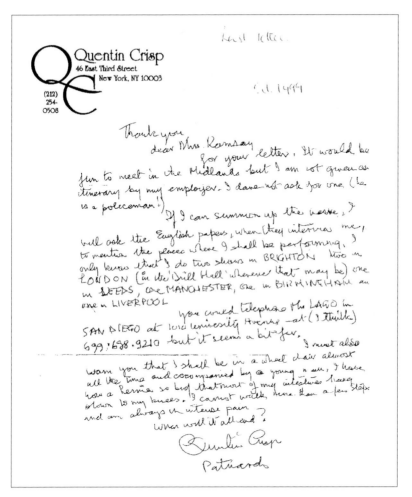

QUENTIN'S LAST LETTER, TO HIS NIECE, FRANCES: 'I MUST ALSO WARN YOU
THAT I SHALL BE IN A WHEELCHAIR ALMOST ALL THE TIME AND ACCOMPANIED
BY A YOUNG MAN. I HAVE NOW A HERNIA SO BIG THAT MOST OF MY INTESTINES
HANG DOWN TO MY KNEES. I CANNOT WALK MORE THAN A FEW STEPS AND AM
ALWAYS IN INTENSE PAIN. WHEN WILL IT ALL END?'

Just pop me in a black bin bag

When I'm dead I don't want a fuss, just pop me in a black bin bag and put me out with the rubbish.

On 9 January 2000, BBC radio broadcast *Resident Alien* on Radio 3 as a tribute to Quentin. In March 2000, almost a year to the day since I had last visited him in his East Third Street apartment, I returned to New York to speak at his memorial held near his old home in the historic Cooper Union Building in the heart of New York's East Village. It was a remarkable affair. In the hall where Abraham Lincoln had once delivered his historic 'might makes right' speech which propelled him to the White House in 1860, almost 1,000 people gathered to hear tributes to him. Everyone from rich Upper East Side ladies in mink stoles to downtown leather boys in riding chaps, from workmen to politicians, heard speaker after speaker come to the podium behind a small forestage – set with his trademark chair and table and the obligatory glass of Scotch on it – to pay tribute to him.

The actor John Hurt, spoke of Quentin as 'one of the truly great figures of the 20th century'. He said, 'He was a true philosopher and the only philosopher who actually lived his own philosophy,' who 'was born into impossibility and never wavered from his personal crusade.' He said, 'The soft light of his sunset enriched all our lives.' They heard his on-stage collaborator and long-standing friend, the performance artist Penny Arcade, say Quentin 'grew up to be himself and that's the greatest thing anyone can hope to achieve'; and Louis Colaianni, director of the Quentin Crisp Museum, which bizarrely resides in a flat in Kansas City and contains Quentin's first typewriter and a lock of his hair, call him the 'Lower East Side Mother Teresa'. Tom Steele, the author and publisher, said Quentin had 'one of the most focused identities of our time'; and Ned Rorem said that 'with his death the world weighs less'. His surviving relatives, who Crisp seldom mentioned to others, talked of 'Uncle

Quentin', of his warmth and generosity, and of how his public image as a 'sad lonely embittered old queen' who wasn't interested in anything that interested anyone else (his own words) was at odds with the gentle man who had attended their weddings and christenings and upstaged everyone with his outrageous appearance. This was perhaps the most surprising element of the evening. Quentin always gave the impression he had no family. He seldom talked about them and except for the book of his early life, *The Naked Civil Servant*, almost never wrote about them and yet it emerged he kept in regular contact with people on both sides of the Atlantic.

In England his niece, Frances Ramsay, recalls visiting Quentin when she was just a girl and having a meal with him in the St Pancras Hotel at which the waiter was so shocked by Quentin's appearance that he fell backwards shattering glass everywhere, and she still has many letters from him including the one where he wrote to inform her he was no longer to be referred to as Denis but had become Quentin Crisp.

It also emerged that shortly after arriving in New York, in 1980, Quentin's great niece, Michèle Goycoolea, made contact with Quentin and came from her New Jersey home with her mother to meet him. They got on well and she loved having a famous relative. As the years went by and she married and had a family Quentin became a regular visitor to her house for family occasions. Michelle has many fond recollections of the visits of 'Uncle Quentin'. Unfortunately she has no secrets to tell. She received much the same performance as everyone else and was seldom able to engage in what she called 'conventional conversation'. That said, the family loved his visits where he would sit and chat to the children and regale them with stories of his celebrity life. I asked her if he ever brought gifts for the children, she said, 'No and he never paid for anything.' He was nothing if not consistent.

Also at the memorial was Professor Eric Bentley, the writer, critic and academic, who whilst saying how much he had ultimately admired Quentin because he was 'one of the toughest, strongest men he'd ever known' hinted at the other side of the man. He remembered the time Quentin declared to the world's press at the height of the Aids epidemic that he 'didn't believe in it' and how, at the height of the prominence of the gay liberation movement when sex with as many partners as possible was not only desirable but a political statement, he declared that 'sex was the last refuge of the miserable'.

There's no doubt Quentin Crisp was a huge paradox: he was a man who existed in almost total obscurity for 50 years before becoming famous almost overnight and yet who refused to live in anything except abject squalor. A man who was a regular on television and a required guest at the opening of society events and film premieres and yet who never removed his name from the New York phone directory. A man who was so quintessentially English that the singer Sting could write a hit song about him entitled *Englishman in New York* and yet who never tired of declaring that England was a 'terrible place, where no-one is your friend'. A man who could claim to care only about the underdog in one breath and yet ask why President Clinton sent 'the brave and the beautiful' to Yugoslavia in the next, saying he should 'let them die, they are only Europeans'. A man who did as much as anyone to forward the cause of gay rights and yet who never tired in telling anyone who would listen that the life of a homosexual was 'horrible'. And a man who said he went on working because he had to and yet who left a small fortune to relatives who few knew he had.

This was a man whose life had spanned most of the 20th century. A man born in the shadow of Victoria and the trial of Oscar Wilde, who died in the meek twilight of the Clinton years. Who had survived two world wars, seen men jailed for sleeping with other men, the legalisation of gay marriage, a government installed in Britain with three gay Cabinet Ministers and at the end of the century the crucifixion of a Texas teenager by his classmates for being gay. A man who lived for almost 50 years as a social outcast in near poverty on the streets of London in which he was born, and had then risen to become one of the most visible gay figures in the world and the natural heir to Oscar Wilde, before going on to be rejected by many in the gay movement as reactionary and homophobic. A man who, at 70, left his tiny room in Chelsea for the wilder shores of New York's East Village and who, on arriving at John F Kennedy international airport and being asked the obligatory, 'Have you anything to declare?' replied, 'Only my sin.' Who, after a brief sojourn at the Chelsea Hotel during which Nancy Spungen died, found a tiny room in a rooming house hard on the Bowery where he lived for 20 years alongside winos and drug addicts and a chapter of the Hell's Angels. Who, in his new life in New York, became even more prominent, performing his one-man show, going on to write more books and a diary, and being featured in television documentaries and on countless TV shows, and who developed a reputation for going to every opening he was invited to.

He was a flirt and a tease, a conservative and a left-wing radical, an icon and an iconoclast, an Edwardian gentleman and a revolutionary, a hater of the establishment and yet an upholder of many of his values. He simultaneously struggled to belong whilst always distancing himself from getting too close to anyone, never failing to address even those close to him as Miss or Mr. In short he was a great glittering contradiction.

His history was to a large extent a history of homosexuality in the 20th century. The journey from being beaten on the streets of London to being laughed at as passé and reactionary by other gays mirrored the changing attitudes of 100 years of gay history. He was the last great link to Wilde. He was a fervent individualist and the line − 'Ask yourself if there were no praise and no blame who would I be then, then you know who you are and what your style is.' − will echo down through the ages. His death captured in it the essence of his life: the desire to please, the craving for the spotlight, the need to remain in control and the absolute commitment, despite all his self-deprecation, to significance.

The sissy from the suburbs ended his life as one of the iconic figures of the 20th century and he did it by documenting with candour, strength and generosity the struggle that had been his life. He turned pain into humour and anger into wit. He embraced life as a great metaphysical joke to which the only logical response was laughter. He left behind him a minor masterpiece in *The Naked Civil Servant* but, as important as his writing, he left behind him an essence so distinct that like Oscar Wilde and Noel Coward before him, his very name conjures up an attitude and a philosophy to deal with the business of living.

I thought I knew at nine years' old in the playground of my school watching my friend fall off the tree stump what the words 'Quentin Crisp' meant. Twenty-three years later I realise how much more than a merely gay icon he was. A passionate individualist, he had a brilliant mind and in many respects a genuinely visionary outlook. His words will continue to resonate down the ages because they speak of eternal truths, something of the essence of what it is to be human. Time will be kind to Quentin Crisp and the success of *Resident Alien – The Play* in New York (winning Bette Bourne an OBIE Award) earlier this year and the play's continued production around the world along with the publication of his final book, *Dusty Answers*, by his friend Phillip Ward, will introduce a whole new generation of people to his genius. To the delicious bunch of misfits in our societies that make the world a more colourful place Quentin Crisp will always be a patron saint. As Penny Arcade said, 'He grew up to be himself, and that's the greatest thing anyone can hope to achieve.'

FAMILY PHOTOS: TOP: WITH BABA AND NIECE, FRANCES;
MIDDLE–LEFT: WITH NIECE, ELAINE; MIDDLE–RIGHT: AT GREAT–NIECE, MICHÈLE'S
WEDDING;
BOTTOM–LEFT, MIDDLE AND RIGHT: WITH THREE OF HIS GREAT–GREAT–NEPHEWS

> 129 Beaufort Street,
> LONDON   S. W. 3.
> FLAxman 9398
>
> 11th. August '81

Thank you,
>   dear Mrs. Ramsay,
>   for your kind letter. I'll
catch the coach that leaves Victoria Coach Station at
10 o'clock on Monday, the 31st. of August.
>   Sad to say,
I shall have to leave on the Wednesday in order to be
in Preston on the Thursday of that week.
>   Everything has
become very difficult; I must leave England forever on
Sunday, the 13th. of September as the smiling and nodding
racket must begin earlier than I was originally told.

>   Looking forward to witnessing you all.

>   QUENTIN CRISP

A FEW LAST WORDS...

46 East 3rd. Street,
NEW YORK   10003
212:254:0508

30th. December '85

Thank you,
       all,
              for your kind Christmas card.
It was nice to know that you have all gone on
living and, presumably, flourishing.
                                   I have
done the same in a muted sort of a way. I've
given up writing books -- an occupation that I
never really liked because it takes me away from
people who, especially since I came here, are my
chief pastime. I still write articles for various
magazines including one in the middle of Brighton
whither I went last Spring to 'do' the festival
there.
              It would be nice to see you all again
but, apart from that pleasure, I do not really
long to visit England; it now seems a long way
off. I still hear from some strangers there --
especially when an interview was shown on television in which I tried to explain The Lower East
Side of Manhattan to a certain Mr. Harty. Into
my room here, which is smaller than my room in
England was, came Mr. Harty, his producer, a
continuity girl, a cameraman, a sound expert
and an assistant. The situation was somewhat
stressful but we all survived and spent a second
day wandering along St. Mark's Place to the
amusement of the natives.
                            I spend quite a lot
of time on television here because there is so
much television time to fill in that anyone who
will chatter is welcome. Of course I say the
same things in the same way but no one seems to
care. Perhaps they don't listen.
                                   I see Mrs.
Goycooleya and family from time to time; they all
seem well and happy though, apparently, they long
to go to Brussels for some unknown reason.
                                            Of
Mrs. Brenner I have not heard.
                                   I survived the
embarrassments of Christmas unharmed and hope
that you all did the same.
                            Happy New Year. . .

19th. December '90

Thank you,
        dear Mrs. Ramsay,
                        for your
kind card. How glorious the picture
made the coast of Devon look!
                        I am
sorry that I couldn't do anything for
the second Mr. Ramsay to facilitate his
sojourn among the mahogany trees but I
really don't know Mr. Sting. I only
once worked for him. He appeared here
in the Threepenny Opera but it was off
before I could find anyone rich enough
to buy me a seat.
                    I'm struggling on
and now write a sort of diary for a
kinky paper in New York. This not only
entails more typing but also more going
to places and meeting people so as to
have something about which to write.
                                    I'm
being sent to Seattle next month   almost as great a journey as going to England but less of an upheaval.
                        I send
my best wishes to the entire family.

                    Doris

I'm sorry Mrs. Thatcher's acid reign is
over: she was a star.

                    46 East 3rd. Street,
                    NEW YORK   10003
                    212:254:0508

                    15th. August '91

Thank you,
        dear Mrs. Ramsay,
                        for your kind letter.
It's good of you to be concerned about my eczema.
It is true that your friend telephoned me and that
I mentioned my affliction. It is perpetual and in-
curable but it doesn't prevent me from doing whatever has to be done. I still flit about the continent. Last week I went to Los Angeles to be in
a television programme ruled by Mr. Reagan's son
and next week I shall fly to Boston to introduce a
new documentary film about me called RESIDENT ALIEN.
It needs no introduction but, as you probably know,
the personality business -- the smiling and nodding
racket -- is all the rage here.
                            If Mr. Ramsay Two
arrives in New York, I will make great efforts to
see him. Whether he can stay with the Crawfords I
have no idea; I have visited their home more than
once but cannot recall how large it is. He is quite
probably willing to sleep on someone's bathroom
floor.
        I was told by Mrs Goycöolea that you had
sold the shop but she did not give me your newest
address. I'm delighted that you are enjoying your
retirement; I never understood what English newspapers called ' the problem of retirement' but then,
as you know, I retired at birth.
                            I now receive just
over five hundred dollars a month from Mr. Bush for
some unknown reason so I am doing all right.

        Best wishes to all of you,

                QUENTIN CRISP

QUENTIN CRISP AND TIM FOUNTAIN

The Sunday Correspondent Questionnaire

Published in *The Sunday Correspondent* magazine, 24 September 1989.

WHAT IS YOUR IDEA OF PERFECT HAPPINESS?
To live in the continuous present.

WHERE WOULD YOU LIKE TO LIVE?
Manhattan.

WHAT WAS YOUR GREATEST ACT OF COURAGE?
Being born.

WHAT IS YOUR GREATEST FEAR?
Poverty.

ON WHICH OCCASIONS DO YOU LIE?
When asked what I think of anyone.

WHICH TALENT WOULD YOU MOST LIKE TO HAVE?
A talent for making money.

WHO ARE YOUR FAVOURITE FICTIONAL CHARACTERS
None.

WITH WHICH HISTORICAL FIGURE DO YOU MOST IDENTIFY?
None.

WHAT IS YOUR FAVOURITE BUILDING?
The bank.

WHAT WOULD YOUR MOTTO BE?
If at first you don't succeed, failure may be your style.

WHICH LIVING WOMEN DO YOU MOST ADMIRE?
Elizabeth Taylor because she is so beautiful, so rich and so courageous in fighting her many illnesses and because she is wonderfully funny, something for which she never gets any credit.

WHICH LIVING MAN DO YOU MOST ADMIRE?
Can't think of one.

WHAT IS THE TRAIT YOU MOST DEPLORE IN OTHERS?
Unreliability.

WHAT IS YOUR GREATEST EXTRAVAGANCE?
My television set.

WHAT BORES YOU?
Nothing.

WHAT MAKES YOU MOST DEPRESSED?
Lack of money.

WHAT IS YOUR FAVOURITE COLOUR?
Black.

WHAT IS YOUR FAVOURITE ANIMAL?
Hate them all.

WHAT IS YOUR FAVOURITE BIRD?
Hate them all.

WHAT IS YOUR FAVOURITE FLOWER?
Hate them all.

WHAT IS YOUR FAVOURITE WORD?
Money.

WHO IS YOUR FAVOURITE PROSE WRITER?
Damon Runyan.

WHO IS YOUR FAVOURITE POET?
Tennyson.

WHAT OBJECTS DO YOU ALWAYS CARRY WITH YOU?
Keys and cash.

WHAT IS YOUR FAVOURITE JOURNEY?
Coming home.

WHAT IS YOUR FAVOURITE NAME?
Quentin Crisp.

WHO IS YOUR FAVOURITE PAINTER?
Mr Hockney.

WHO ARE YOUR FAVOURITE MUSICIANS?
Hate music.

WHICH LIVING PERSON DO YOU MOST DESPISE?
None.

WHAT DO YOU CONSIDER THE MOST OVERRATED VIRTUE?
Aggressiveness.

WHICH WORDS OR PHRASES DO YOU MOST OVERUSE?
I.

WHAT WOULD YOUR CHOSEN NATIONALITY BE?
American.

WHEN AND WHERE WERE YOU HAPPIEST?
Here and now.

HOW WOULD YOU LIKE TO DIE?
Soon.

WHAT DO YOU MOST DISLIKE ABOUT YOUR APPEARANCE?
Old age.

HOW WOULD YOU LIKE TO BE REMEMBERED?
I don't care.

WHAT KEEPS YOU AWAKE AT NIGHT?
Nothing.

WHO WOULD YOU MOST LIKE TO HAVE BEEN?
Nobody.

WHAT IS YOUR PRESENT STATE OF MIND?
Calm.

Bibliography

The Naked Civil Servant
by Quentin Crisp
How to Become a Virgin
by Quentin Crisp
How to Go to the Movies
by Quentin Crisp
The Stately Homo
edited by Paul Bailey
The Wit and Wisdom of Quentin Crisp
edited by Guy Kettelhack with Quentin Crisp

Picture credits

Page 8
Photograph copyright © by Joseph Mulligan. All rights reserved.
Page 18, 24, 124, 136, 152, 175, 181-185
From the Pratt family private collection
Page 148, 156, 160
Bruce Hart
Page 162, 164
From the play *Resident Alien*
Page 186
Tim Fountain

The publishers would like to thank Michèle Crawford for her permission to reproduce letters and family photographs. Thanks also to Phillip Ward for his help with securing photographic permissions (www.crisperanto.org), and to Bruce Hart, for the last-minute sharing of his photographs.